Creativity & Innovation

Ideas for
Enterprising Managers

Other Mercury books by Matthew Archer:

Call Yourself a Manager!
Fit for Business

Ideas for Enterprising Managers

MATTHEW ARCHER

MERCURY BOOKS
Published by W.H. Allen & Co. Plc

Copyright © 1988 Matthew Archer

All rights reserved. No part of this publication may be reproduced, stored in a retrieval system, or transmitted in any form or by any means, electronic, mechanical, photocopying, recording, or otherwise without the prior permission of the publishers.

First published in 1988
by the Mercury Books Division of
W.H. Allen & Co. Plc
44 Hill Street, London W1X 8LB

Set in Palatino by Phoenix Photosetting
Printed and bound in Great Britain by
Mackays of Chatham PLC, Chatham, Kent

This book is sold subject to the condition that it shall not, by way of trade or otherwise, be lent, re-sold, hired out or otherwise circulated without the publisher's prior consent in any form of binding or cover other than that in which it is published and without a similar condition including this condition being imposed upon the subsequent purchaser.

British Library Cataloguing in Publication Data

Archer, Matthew.
 Ideas for enterprising managers
 1. Management. Techniques
 I. Title
 658.4

ISBN 1 85251 041 2

CONTENTS

Introduction   7

Part 1   *Efficiency and Effectiveness*

1. Improving Performance – A Broad-Brush Checkover   11
2. Planning and Control   25
3. Creativity – Solving the Insoluble   36
4. Making the Impossible Decision   41
5. Getting the Organisational Structure Right – Nine Aspects to Look At   44
6. Are Your Stock Records Really Necessary?   58
7. Cutting the Cost of Cost Control   62
8. Solving Complicated Problems   66
9. The Price of Meetings   73

Part 2   *The People Asset*

10. Staff Selection   79
11. Making Appraisal Schemes Work   87
12. Training – Selling the Idea   96
13. Setting Up On-Job Training   99

14.	Getting Over the Delegation Problem	110
15.	Questions of Discipline	115
16.	The Manager's Time	120

Part 3 *The Paperwork Obstacle*

17.	The Fight Against Forms	127
18.	Unclogging the Paperwork Drain	136
19.	Reducing Clerical Errors	143
20.	Office Mechanisation – Points to Watch	148
21.	Finding Time to Read	152
22.	Cutting Down on Reports	154

Part 4 *Help from Simple Maths*

23.	Break-Even Point – And its Uses	163
24.	Pinpointing the Problem (or Opportunity)	170
25.	Activity Sampling – Finding Out What Really Goes On	173
26.	Forecasting the Likelihood of . . .	182
27.	Spotting the Trend	186

Index 191

INTRODUCTION

An 'enterprising' manager is one who is never entirely content with the status quo. He is always looking for new ideas to improve his own performance and that of his staff. But he has little time to spare for reading long and highly specialised textbooks.

In the earlier days, particularly throughout the 1960s and 1970s, an Organisation and Methods department could be found in virtually every medium to large company – and in some small ones as well. The O & M service provided support to line managers. Enterprising line managers would ask the O & M analysts to take a good look at their department, identify problems and come up with ideas. Every professional O & M department had a 'kit' of techniques and analytical methods which they used to support the line managers. Now that the O & M function has been largely superseded by the principle of managers taking full responsibility for the effectiveness of their departments, these techniques and methods have, to some extent, been forgotten. The modern tendency is for companies seeking ideas to employ the consulting side of a large firm of accountants to solve their problems. The result is that the only problems looked at are the corporate ones, which are obvious to top management, leaving the line manager with little support. In addition, the accounting-orientated consultant is also likely to be accounts-orientated in the service he provides. Emphasis falls on the more esoteric areas of tax, financial planning, share issues, mergers and the like.

The ideas in this book – all tried and tested in real life – are designed to meet at least some of the more down-to-earth needs of the enterprising line manager – to give him a do-it-yourself kit for improving his own performance and that of his department.

The first chapter describes an overview approach focusing on the likely problems and opportunities for improvement. Whilst suggestions for action are given for each of the 14 areas suggested for examination, further detail and expansion of the ideas is given in subsequent chapters.

Each subsequent chapter covers a specific subject. Wherever the ideas are based on techniques, mathematical or otherwise, these techniques have been simplified so that the enterprising manager can achieve the optimum result, i.e. some useful action which is not prolonged or complicated by non-essential finer points.

The rather cumbersome practice of writing 'his or hers', 'him or her', 'he or she' has been left out for ease of reading. In all cases references to gender should be read as including both sexes.

Thanks are due to the magazine *International Management* for agreement to use modifications of articles which have appeared in the magazine for Chapters 8 and 20.

Part 1

Efficiency and Effectiveness

The nine chapters of Part 1 are not intended to cover *every* aspect of management which relates to efficiency and effectiveness but are nevertheless designed to give the enterprising manager a good, practical range of ideas for improving quality and quantity of work.

If the manager uses his imagination, he will see how, with some modification, many of the ideas and principles can be applied in a variety of situations. In other words, if the ideas are treated as such (and not as rules) a lot can be achieved.

1

IMPROVING PERFORMANCE – A BROAD-BRUSH CHECKOVER

From time to time the enterprising manager will want to take a critical look at the performance of the operation he is responsible for. Ideally the manager will decide to do this on a regular basis without being prompted. When things are going wrong and the boss is complaining it may be too late. Managers, often up to their necks in pressures and problems, sometimes wonder where to begin such a review. This chapter provides a checklist of things to be looked at to ensure a continuing good performance or to improve performance. It is rare that improvements cannot be found, however satisfactory things may seem to be. Working through the checklist which follows is very likely to be time well spent. Ideally each topic will be reviewed regularly – say every six months – as a way to avoid gradual and perhaps unnoticed deterioration in some aspect of the department's work.

Job conditions

In the final analysis everything depends on the employees. If they are not happy work will suffer. It is therefore more than a question of humanity to make sure that job conditions are good. The following are some of the aspects which should be examined:

IDEAS FOR ENTERPRISING MANAGERS

1. Physical conditions

- Are the work places clean, comfortable and adequately lit?

- Is protective clothing provided, where necessary, to meet legal, safety and comfort requirements?

- Are conditions conducive to safe working?

- Are working hours and holidays fair and reasonable?

- Are people provided with decent services such as good canteen meals, clean lavatories and accessible and efficient first aid?

- Is equipment and furniture in good order and suited to the job or purpose?

One factor which can cause working conditions to be neglected is that good conditions will not motivate people to greater effort or achievement. However, bad conditions positively *demotivate* people and give rise to grumbling and a generally lacklustre attitude. Providing good, clean, safe and fair conditions plays an essential part in ensuring a *contented* workforce.

It is a fortunate manager who has in his own hands the authority (and the budget) to correct any deficiencies in working conditions. More often someone else has the power and the money and it is the manager's job to bring any deficiencies to their attention.

One manager, unable to influence his company's office administration manager, persuaded the managing director to visit his department. The cramped and scruffy conditions were only too evident to the M.D. and some of the less obvious problems such as obsolete and unreliable equipment were pointed out. The M.D. was particularly impressed by a young clerk who told him that she was

Improving performance – a broad-brush checkover

continually being blamed for missing documents when she had no proper place to store them and no work surface on which to sort them. The manager in turn pointed out the cost and delays caused by missing documents – cost being a subject close to the M.D's heart. The result was a substantial refurbishment and new up-to-date equipment.

Managers can also bring pressure to bear on those who hold the purse strings by preparing and submitting a statement of the estimated costs of poor conditions. These can include:

- *Staff turnover.* The losses in terms of disruption, recruitment and training could be significant.

- *Absenteeism.* An abundance of one and two-day absences for minor (and often mysterious) ailments can result from poor conditions. Bad lighting and constant noise can result in headaches and general malaise. The monthly cost of time lost for such reasons can be a powerful persuader.

- *Errors and delays.* These are particularly significant when customer service is adversely affected. Some statistical evidence might do the trick. Delayed invoicing is a specific example which managers should look out for as this has a direct influence on company cash flow.

It is important that the estimated costs are backed up by evidence showing unsatisfactory working conditions to be at least in part to blame. This can be accomplished by recording and reporting specific instances. For example, the number of days work lost due to the failure of an aged minicomputer, or the customer records being removed with the wastepaper because they were piled on the floor.

2. Recruitment, promotion and salaries

Is recruitment professionally done and does the immediate boss have a say in the choice of people? The answer should be 'yes' in both cases if the chance of having square pegs in round holes is to be reduced. One company which only recruited high-fliers and imposed the choice on line managers suffered markedly high turnover of new employees. Eventually, it was realised that staff selection should be geared to the nature of the work and that line managers were in the best position to ensure that people would fit in.

Is there a clear promotion policy which will motivate staff and encourage them? For example, if supervisory and management vacancies are always filled by external recruitment the existing staff will be discouraged. Such a policy also raises questions about the training of staff, or lack of it.

Are salaries determined by a system that is seen to be fair and are the salaries at least comparable with those of other employees in similar jobs elsewhere? Determining salaries by arbitrary methods or on the basis of 'what the traffic will bear' is asking for trouble and accusations of favouritism. The line manager who is aware of deficiencies in the areas of recruitment, promotion and salaries must, if he can do nothing directly on his own authority, bring the problem to the attention of those who can. Chapters 13, 14 and 15 deal with delegation, appraisal schemes and staff selection. They will provide some ideas and, if needed, some ammunition.

3. Skills and training

Are there many inadequacies in the skills of people, e.g. how many people are struggling to cope with the job or doing it badly?

What training is needed to correct inadequacies?

Is there a training plan to deal with the problem or is training done on an expediency basis – or not at all?

Ideas for action on the subject of skills and training are given in Chapters 10, 11 and 12. It is in the interests of the manager to see that what should be done is done in this area for the reasons explained in these later chapters.

4. Leadership

Is the manager's own style of leadership good enough?

- Staff should be relaxed and communicate easily and readily with the boss. Do they? If not, the manager must examine his own style.
  The manager must, as far as humanly possible, make a conscious effort to be receptive to ideas and complaints coming from staff. It is only too easy when tired and under pressure to give an unfriendly response to a suggestion – even a good one. The unsympathetic response can result in hurt feelings and anger which will inhibit future communication. Young and inexperienced people are particularly vulnerable to the sharp rebuff and all their natural enthusiasm is turned into resentment.

- The boss should encourage and support – not 'motivate' by threats and fear. How much time is spent in 'support sessions'?
  Since people are the main resource which the manager has at his disposal he should spend *at least* 25 per cent of his time coaching, encouraging and helping.

- Everyone should know what is going on and what the company expects: the problems to be solved and so on. How many people are aware of departmental objectives for example?

- Staff should be consulted by the boss for ideas, opinions and objectives. How frequently does consultation take place? Anything less than a weekly exchange between the individual and his immediate boss is too little. There are some exceptions to this rule of thumb where, for example, someone is working on a project as opposed to day-to-day 'production'. In cases where results are not expected for a long time the consultation needed may be less than in a fast moving situation. However, it is better to err on the side of having 'too much' consultation rather than too little.

Managers should carry out a little self-assessment from time to time considering some of the above points and asking themselves such further questions as:

- Are my staff happy and enthusiastic? Are any of them sullen and 'difficult'? Why?

- Do my staff communicate *willingly* with me and each other or is it just a one-way process with me issuing orders?

- Do my staff work as a team (e.g. giving each other a hand when needed) or are they just a collection of individuals?

- Am I aware of the problems and difficulties of my staff and, if so, now much help do I give them?

- Am I 'too busy' to pay much attention to my staff, their work and their performance?

- How often do I praise and encourage and how often administer a 'kick in the pants'?

- What can I do to make myself a more effective leader?

Note: A worthwhile book which deals with this topic in detail is *The Human Organisation* by Rensis Likert, published by McGraw-Hill. Likert, who made a detailed study of what is needed to be a good leader, offers some helpful and interesting advice.

5. Objectives

Has the manager agreed objectives (and standards) with his staff and colleagues? Are these objectives clear and measurable (e.g. to reduce wastage by 15 per cent by January 1st) and known and understood by all the staff? In other words, do we clearly know where we are going and how we will get there?

Some managers keep their objectives, or the objectives placed on them from above, as close to their chests as they would a state secret. They then expect their staff to achieve these unknown objectives with enthusiasm. Making sure that everyone knows what the objectives are is a basic part of good leadership and an exercise in common sense. If everyone knows what they are expected to achieve they have a better chance of doing so – which is of direct benefit to the manager himself.

It can be a useful (and instructive) exercise for the manager to make a point of asking his staff from time to time what objectives have been set for the department and the individual. Even if the objectives have, as they should, been provided in writing, the question will often reveal ignorance or misunderstanding of them. Should this be the case it is the manager's fault. A conscious effort is required to improve this particular form of communication in future, by careful and patient explanation.

6. Organisational Structure

Is the structure right or are there problems caused by over large groups, inadequate supervision etc.? The organisational structure is a 'framework' for good management. If the structure is wrong, good management becomes difficult or impossible. A number of organisational aspects are discussed in Chapter 5 with some ideas for improvements when the situation is seen to be unsatisfactory.

7. Methods

How long is it since work methods – paperwork, processes, technology – were critically examined?

If more than a year ago, it is likely that improvements can be made. Out-of-date records, forms and paperwork in general are time-wasting and cause errors. There may also be new technology which can profitably be taken on board. The six chapters in Part 3 deal with the many problems which need to be looked at from time to time. The symptoms of these problems include:

- Frequent and repeated clerical errors.
- Bottlenecks.
- Delays in producing or completing paperwork.
- Neglected work, e.g. the 'I didn't receive the pink copy' syndrome.
- Repeated recording of the same information.

Should any of these symptoms be in evidence a good look at methods is indicated.

8. Equipment

Is everyone provided with good, up-to-date and reliable equipment? Is work being done by muscle and sweat which could be made easier by supplying equipment designed to take the load? Even a wheelbarrow might save a lot of work and aggravation. Word processors might be worthwhile where lots of typing (and retyping) is involved. Even a small computer.

Is there any old and battered equipment which is inefficient or subject to frequent breakdowns?

9. Manpower

Is manpower planned or does the company drift along finding itself with insufficient people of the right type? Is there a succession plan to fill the gap when older employees retire – with training having been carried out in anticipation of this? Are the right type of people being employed? For example, are selection standards unnecessarily high? This can result in high turnover from boredom.

10. Work loads

Is work allocated to a plan? Is work allocated fairly and effectively or are there pockets of underemployment alongside overloaded people?

A good look at who does what can yield interesting and profitable results and no manager should kid himself that he always knows what is going on in the department. A review of the type and volume of work done by each individual can reveal imbalance or even serious unfairness in the allocation of responsibility. A review can lead to improved output as a result of making use of underemployment time and elimination of bottlenecks.

11. Responsibility and authority

Is there a clear allocation of responsibility and does adequate authority go with it? Does *everyone* know who is responsible for what? Are there any areas where no one seems to be responsible?

Any lack of clarity in the allocation of responsibility can result in work being neglected and disruptive quarrelling. Ideally everyone will have a well written and regularly updated job description written *jointly* by the manager and the employee.

12. Control

Is there a procedure for control – in particular a procedure which employees themselves operate? For example, can the employees themselves judge whether output is good enough in terms of quality and quantity? Can they – as well as the boss – see problems building up in time to take avoiding action? The best control systems are normally the visual ones such as planning boards, wall charts and even clearly marked piles of pending work and work completed. The ability to see the situation at a glance is helpful to both manager and staff.

Complicated records should be avoided if possible as these create even more paperwork and are often full of errors. One warehouse kept detailed card index records showing goods received, storage location, despatches and so on. The warehouse manager was the only person allowed to fill in the various movements on the cards and he was often behind in this time-consuming task. There was, in addition, no guarantee that dockets indicating stock movements would be accurately completed or sent to the manager promptly – or at all. The records became more and more out of date with the result that the production planning department started their own, duplicate system of recording. This record was also found to be unreliable and neither record made any sense when tested by physical stock checking.

The whole recording system was scrapped and replaced by a visual system in which the *stock itself* amounted to the record. In other words, if there were two piles of pallets each five pallets high any number of staff who could see them knew at a glance that the stock was 10 pallets worth. (See Chapter 6 for more on this.)

13. Communication

This forms a part of the leadership style but is important enough to warrant special attention.

Improving performance – a broad-brush checkover

Are the staff well and thoroughly informed by management or is it left to shop stewards and rumours? Do staff communicate upwards and sideways? What are people told and not told?

Everyone ought to be efficiently informed of everything possible as this will encourage interest in the job and discourage damaging speculation and misunderstanding.

There was a British company which, with the best intentions, introduced a profit-related incentive scheme. Properly handled this scheme would have benefited both the company and the employees but it was very poorly explained with the result that the employees were opposed to it. After a number of complaints the company promised a written and comprehensive explanation of how the scheme worked. Incredibly, this explanation was never given because the director responsible considered it unnecessary! The scheme was abandoned and not only was a good opportunity lost but a great deal of bitterness was left behind since no one had dispelled the view that the whole thing was an attempted con-trick.

On a smaller scale the same damage can be caused at departmental level. The enterprising manager will ensure that at least his own communications are good and his methods effective.

The commonplace means of communication such as notices and bulletin boards and circulars to all staff are rarely satisfactory as means to communicate effectively. Bulletin boards are often untidy and plastered with ancient notices. They are sometimes situated in out of the way places and, even if not, many people ignore them.

Circulars to staff are capable of misinterpretation and are sometimes written in a style designed, not to communicate effectively, but to demonstrate the cleverness of the author. Jargon can be found in circulars which may be impressive to some people but is incomprehensible to others. The real value of this form of attempted communication was illustrated outside a factory (now closed down) where the exit road was littered with thrown-away copies of an important message to employees. One departing employee was asked why he had thrown his copy away. 'Don't understand it mate', was his reply.

The best solution to the problem is the regular face-to-face meeting where the manager and his team get together. The manager can not only pass on information in terms which people will understand, he can also put the message in the context of the department and its work. The meeting gives an opportunity for the staff to ask questions and, no less important, feed back opinions and information to the manager. In other words, the communication is in both directions. At the same time employees will be able to make their views known to each other, thus creating the ideal situation in which communication is up, down and sideways.

Such meetings need not be lengthy. In one company each manager (and in the case of large departments, each supervisor) has a 10-minute meeting with the people directly reporting to them *every* morning. These meetings, which are conducted standing up to discourage unnecessary discussion, cover the following:

- Any particular problems, targets or other matters to be dealt with on that day.

- Company messages, e.g. arrangements for bank holiday skeleton staff, changes to security arrangements, health screening, etc.

- Points which employees may wish to raise – some of which may be discussed at greater length by the manager and the employee concerned after the meeting.

- Individual or departmental progress items such as output or sales figures.

An alternative arrangement adopted in a company department with less day-to-day activity is a weekly meeting lasting about two hours. This meeting takes place every Friday afternoon when the six members of the department review with their manager the week's events. Problems are discussed and suggestions are encouraged from individuals to find solutions both for departmental objectives and for those of individuals. The manager passes on information from his superiors and this is discussed. Where necessary queries or suggestions are referred back.

Meetings such as these, which must not be allowed to develop into prolonged and irrelevant debates, can be a valuable means of communication and, at the same time, promote team spirit.

Note: A helpful booklet on this subject is 'The Manager's responsibility for communication' – Number 2 in the *Notes for Managers* series published by The Industrial Society.

14. Help with problems

Are employees helped and supported when things go wrong? Are the younger, less experienced staff given a helping hand when needed or just left to struggle on? Even worse, are they grumbled at?

The enterprising manager will be close to his staff and be sympathetic when problems crop up. A few minutes' practical, patient help is a first-class investment for the future which builds employees' confidence, reduces errors and improves morale and output. These, of course, are some of the results to be expected from good leadership.

It is unlikely that every possible aspect of a department's performance will be improved by working through the 14 points listed above. However, a methodical 'go' at them can hardly fail to reveal ways and means to improve effectiveness. This will be particularly true if each of the 14

IDEAS FOR ENTERPRISING MANAGERS

points is discussed by the manager with his staff. Such discussions will bring out the employees' ideas for better ways to do things and substantially increase their enthusiasm for any changes decided on.

2

PLANNING AND CONTROL

At all levels of management, planning ahead is the means by which the enterprising manager can command the future rather than be commanded by it. Planning (and the necessary forecasting) can warn a manager of possible pitfalls and difficulties *before* they develop. He is thus able to take avoiding action before the crisis occurs and by means of planning can also give the business a competitive edge.

A departmental planning process

A supervisor of an invoicing department has six clerk/typists preparing an average of 60 invoices per day. His output rate is thus 10 invoices per employee per day. The company's products are seasonal, and sales normally increase by 30 per cent in the months of November to January inclusive. The sales forecast for the year indicates increasing sales such that the seasonal peak this year will be around 50 per cent and from February onwards will be 17 per cent higher than normal.

From these figures he can calculate his expected work load, i.e.

October   60 invoices per day
November   90 invoices per day

December	90 invoices per day
January	90 invoices per day
February	70 invoices per day
March	70 invoices per day
and so on	

Completing these quantities of invoices (on time) becomes his main departmental objective. To cope with this work load he will need the following staff:

October	6 (his normal team)
November	9
December	9
January	9
February	7
March	7

The supervisor now knows that he can cope satisfactorily in October but will be in trouble in the following months. He can consider some alternative courses of action, e.g.

1. Take on three more staff in time for the November rush. This, however, will give him a problem in February when he will be overstaffed.

    Will natural wastage take care of the surplus?

2. Take on one more employee so that he has the right number of staff in February and put up with a backlog.

    Will the company accept a backlog? Invoicing delays cost money.

    Will the staff become demoralised if they have a mountain of work for three months?

3. Take on one more permanent employee plus two temporaries.

Planning and control

Will temporaries give a satisfactory performance? The work must be accurate.

These are some of the possible alternatives and some of the difficulties arising in each case. The supervisor must weigh up the pros and cons of each and decide which scheme best meets the need with least risk or difficulty.

He must of course allow for other factors, e.g.

- When should he recruit?
- Is the right kind of labour hard to find?
- How long will training take?
- Who will do the training?

Having considered these items the supervisor can design a plan. The plan may not be a 100 per cent success and a variety of unexpected problems could arise. Additionally, the sales forecast could be wrong. However, he will have a greater chance of surviving the crisis if he plans ahead. He will be very vulnerable if he does not.

Why planning is neglected

1. Lack of time

The lack of time may itself be due to failure to plan in the past.

Managers must make time to plan and regard it as an essential part of their jobs.

2. Planning can be hard work

A positive act of willpower is required to go through the planning process. It is very tempting to leave it and hope the problem will solve itself or disappear. It will not, it will probably grow worse!

3. Plans do not always work and the manager is discouraged

This reaction is entirely understandable. But a part of being a good manager is having the tenacity to have another go. It is unrealistic to assume that all plans will be successful as they are largely based on forecasts of future events. The forecasts themselves are not prophecies and will from time to time be wrong.

4. Fear that superiors will not accept the proposals

In fact the only way to produce a cast-iron case is to go through the planning process and present the facts (as far as they can be ascertained) in a logical, objective fashion.

Textbooks on planning tend to be complex and mathematical and many managers are left with the impression that the whole thing is beyond them. In practice business plans should be, and can be, as simple as possible. A few notes on one page of paper is a huge advance from the 'fingers-crossed' position of having no plan at all.

Warning: Beware of external consultants who may sell you a planning system. It will probably consist of 20 beautiful bound volumes of complicated procedures for which you will pay a great deal and never actually find the time to use.

Some necessary steps in planning

Some of these have already been touched on in the invoicing example. The following notes expand the planning steps.

1. Setting objectives

The objectives of the department must be clear, measurable and relevant. There is no point in aiming at a target which is not required to be achieved, which conflicts with other work in the organisation or because of its vagueness can never be compared with performance. For example:

(a) To mail invoices not later than five working days after despatch of the goods. This is a specific target meaning far more than say, 'To mail invoices as soon as possible after despatch'. 'As soon as possible' may be 30 days if only one clerk/typist is employed, or any other time that someone chooses.

(b) To hold sufficient stock to meet two weeks' average despatch. The actual stock quantity required may vary from time to time depending on the level of sales from time to time. In this case the manager must be aware of sales activity and adjust his stock holding accordingly. A simple statement, say, that 100 tonnes must be held in stock is easier to understand but could result in unnecessary expense when business is slack and stock shortages when business is brisk.

2. Forecasting

Managers have no greater powers to foretell the future than anyone else! However, the enterprising manager can make some intelligent guesses, estimates or calculations which will help him. For example:

- What has happened in the past? Did volumes increase at year end last year? If so, how likely is it that the pattern will be repeated?
- Costs have been rising. Will they go on rising?

- Unemployment has been falling. Is there a likelihood of a labour shortage?
- A competitor has just gone out of business. How many of his former customers can be won? How would this affect levels of demand?

Such questions are not always easy to answer but an inspired guess is better than no forecast at all. The uncertainty of the future should not be a deterrent to attempting a forecast.

A real-life dialogue between a production planner and a sales executive illustrates how it is possible to come to helpful conclusions when looking into an uncertain future. The conversation went something like this:

Planner How much do you think the XYZ company will buy from us next year?

Salesman How do I know? It's impossible to see into the future!

Planner You must have some idea.

Salesman I have no idea at all, it all depends on their own sales.

Planner Do you think it will be a million tonnes?

Salesman That's ridiculous! It couldn't possibly be more than 200 tonnes.

Planner Do you think it will be none at all?

Salesman That's very unlikely, they must buy something from us as our competitors could not meet all their demands.

Planner I believe our competitors can produce about 150 tonnes so that would leave XYZ Ltd about 50 tonnes short. Presumably we can expect a 50-tonne order at least?

Planning and control

Salesman Certainly, I would put it nearer 100 tonnes.

Planner So we can be fairly sure of something between 100 and 200 tonnes?

Salesman That sounds about right.

This dialogue continued until a closer range of figures was agreed, leaving the production planner with something to go on rather better than would result from flipping a coin. The story also illustrates the point that many people are tempted to make statements similar to the salesman's first remarks. On closer examination something *can* be done. However little, it is better than nothing.

3. Developing plans

Knowing the objectives and based on the forecast of likely circumstances, the manager can develop alternative ways and means of meeting the objectives. Preferably more than one line of action should be considered and the merits of each weighed up. In considering the alternatives, care must be taken to allow for effects on other sections or departments. Action which may be favourable in one area could cause trouble in another and consultation with colleagues managing other activities is essential. Ideally all major planning will be done on an interdepartmental basis and fit a corporate plan – a situation which the enterprising manager will encourage.

Other factors which must be covered include a timetable of actions (at what times can something be done and what is the best time?). Who should be involved or informed and the best sequence for the various actions must also be considered.

4. Implementation

When the action steps and the timetable have been decided the plan can be launched. However, prior to taking action it is necessary to devise a means to monitor events. Without some way to keep track of progress the plan may go adrift – or, if forecasts were inaccurate, the plan itself may need revision.

The general scheme of things is illustrated in the diagram:

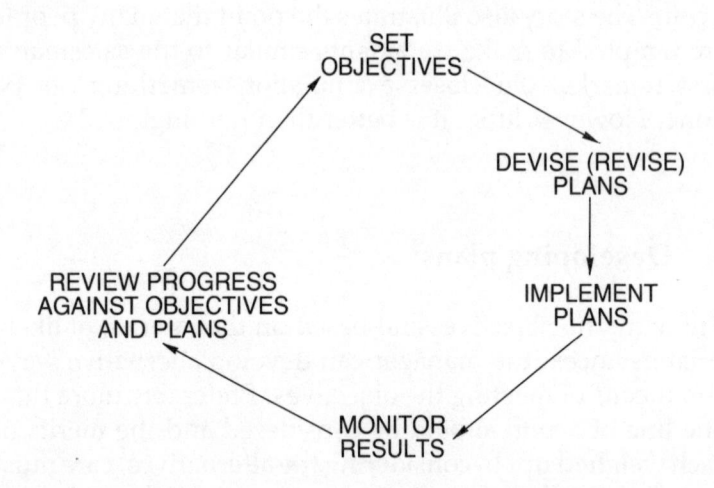

```
         SET
      OBJECTIVES
        ↗        ↘
       /          DEVISE (REVISE)
      /              PLANS
     /                 ↓
  REVIEW PROGRESS   IMPLEMENT
  AGAINST OBJECTIVES  PLANS
  AND PLANS           /
       ↖            ↙
         MONITOR
         RESULTS
```

Our supervisor in the invoicing example was basing his plans on forecast work loads resulting from increased sales. In the event that the increase did not materialise he could end up with an unnecessary increase to his staff. Alternatively, the increase in volume could have been 25 per cent rather than 50 per cent and he would need fewer resources than originally planned.

By monitoring the trend of volumes he may be able to spot inaccuracies early enough to make an adjustment to his plans. He would therefore need to set up a system to keep himself informed as to how sales are going.

Planning and control

Note: It is vitally important to ensure that all concerned are aware of the objectives, the plan, the monitoring system – and why it is all necessary. Failure to communicate this information will result in staff being incapable of taking part effectively and may even cause them to oppose the scheme.

5. Setting up control systems

There are two key elements in designing a control system:

- A 'feedback' procedure.

- A standard for comparison

The feedback procedure is essentially a report of events as they occur. This reporting can include actual sales, actual work produced, costs incurred and the results of any of the action steps in the plan. Particularly important are reports covering time, i.e. performance against the timetable.

The feedback procedure need not be complicated. Commonly used methods in varying situations are:

- Regular and brief meetings at which individuals orally report progress.

- Dockets or vouchers representing work completed. A copy of a despatch or delivery note may be sufficient.

- A chart showing the events to be completed by date. Items are ticked off as completed with the actual date recorded.

- Planning boards with cards or stickers representing actions against a timetable. These can be removed as a job is completed.

Whatever feedback system is chosen it is important to

ensure that progress is reported in time for remedial action to take place if things are going awry. In other words, it is little use being told that, say, purchase of new equipment has not been done on time. The damage has already occurred. If, however, it is known that tenders are late or quotes are slow in coming, this is an early warning of a delay in obtaining new equipment and it may be possible to speed up the process to achieve the final result on target. Thus, on a production line (in offices as well as factories), a report of work completed at each stage of the process can help to ensure that work centres are balanced and the final product will emerge at the right time. Neither too soon nor too late.

A particularly important aspect of early warning is that extra cost may be saved. The nearer to disaster one gets the greater is the likely cost of the remedy.

The standards for comparison are frequently numerical, e.g.

- Cost incurred.

- Time an event occurred.

- Volumes of output.

- Number of staff.

- Stock levels.

In the earlier example there was a standard of 10 invoices per employee per day. If, after recruiting extra staff, the average is running at seven invoices then the objective may not be achieved. Remedial action such as more training or additional equipment will be needed in such a case and the importance of having as much warning as possible is obvious.

Alternatively, an output of 15 invoices per day may remove the necessity for further recruitment at a later stage.

Planning and control

At all events, the manager or supervisor needs a yardstick to measure performance by.

At all levels, from the boardroom to the mailroom the same basic principles apply. Decide the objective, design a plan, implement, monitor and adjust. Of course, it may be necessary to change the objective and start all over again!

3

CREATIVITY – SOLVING THE INSOLUBLE

Managers are sometimes faced with a problem for which there is no apparent solution. Fortunately, there is an easy-to-use technique available to overcome such problems which really does produce results. No particular skills are needed and the method is cheap. The technique is called *brainstorming*.

Brainstorming as a technique should not be confused with the common practice of sitting around in a group clutching coffee cups and wearing worried frowns. Such informal, unstructured gatherings usually end up with expressions of sympathy for the manager who has the problem and not much else. A *disciplined* procedure must be followed which, if properly done, can be a lot of fun *and* gets results.

The process and rules to be followed

1. Assemble a group of intelligent colleagues in a suitable conference room. Include one or two of the 'wild men' in the organisation – those who have a lot to say and not all of it very realistic.

2. Clearly define the problem to be tackled – making sure that everyone fully understands it.

Creativity – solving the insoluble

3. Ask the people present to call out 'solutions' to the problems. These solutions can be as serious or as crazy as they like.

   For example, if someone shouts out 'Burn the factory down' or 'Sue the Bank of England' these ideas should be treated as valid potential solutions!

   It is *vital*, however, that everyone present *absolutely refrains* from criticising a solution, however ridiculous or impractical it may appear. The reason for this restriction is that any criticism or comment will bring the flow of creative thinking to a dead stop and, like most meetings, the session will deteriorate into a totally negative arguing match which leads nowhere.

4. As the solutions are called out write them down on large sheets of paper visible to all. Flip-chart paper stuck to the walls with Blu-tak is a good method. It will be found that each solution will tend to trigger off more. The crazy solutions may well lead to practical ones and this is why they should be visible on the sheets of paper and never criticised.

5. When the ideas run out – usually after about 20 minutes – there should be anything up to 100 solutions written down. These can now be analysed.

6. Having eliminated the impractical (even if attractive) ideas such as assassinating the Managing Director and other unsuitable proposals there will be a residue of possibilities which may well provide the basis of the answer if not the answer itself.

Normally about 10 per cent of the solutions are left for serious consideration. It is not unknown for these to yield a number of real and workable answers to the problem.

A real-life result

Nobody had been able to suggest how to break into a national market governed by regulations barring business with foreign companies. A brainstorming session was organised, lasted 30 minutes and produced 49 ideas. Nine of these ideas were worthy of serious examination and two were used successfully, in practice. A really good brainstorming session can create a new problem – which of the solutions to the insoluble should be adopted. At all events it is an easy technique to use, takes up less time than most meetings – and is a lot more enjoyable.

Evaluating the ideas

Having, as a result of a brainstorming session, compiled a list of solutions it is still necessary to evaluate them so that a final choice can be made. Each solution should be put to a test based on three criteria. Some solutions may fail badly on one or more of the criteria whilst some may pass the test but with varying levels of 'comfort'. The three criteria are:

1. Money and resources

One or more of the solutions may demand too much cash, manpower, machine time or whatever, to be acceptable. There is no point in solving a problem by diverting resources to such a degree that other parts of the business are placed in jeopardy. Each solution being evaluated can be compared in terms of resources needed – some solutions may be eliminated immediately as too expensive and the rest ranked in order.

2. The degree of disturbance

Introducing something new will almost inevitably result in some form of disturbance. Staff may have to be retrained, systems altered, documents redesigned, people relocated, machines shut down or whatever. The degree of such types of disturbance must be estimated and stated and any particularly critical aspects highlighted. The more potentially damaging types of disturbance are those which involve:

- Cash flow problems, e.g. disruption to the collection of debts.

- Reduction, even if temporary, of the level of customer service.

- Damage to staff morale.

- Damage to company image and reputation.

Some of these types of damage may be capable of limitation by various means such as carefully planned publicity and internal communication. The extent to which this can be done must be taken into account.

3. Timing

The implementation of a change may only be possible at a particular time, such as during the summer holiday season or at financial year end. Alternatively, there may be one or two particularly favourable times to make a change. Or the urgency of the problem may demand action immediately.

It is likely that the potential solutions will vary in their time aspect – for example, some will require more preparation for implementation than others. Ideally there will be a solution which fits in with any 'best time' situation.

Having tested each solution against each of the criteria it is likely that one or two will stand out as being better than the rest. Of course, none may be wholly satisfactory and in the end the manager must exercise his judgement in making a choice. There will, inevitably, be some risk involved in any choice, including the choice of doing nothing at all. However, methodically checking out how each solution stands up to the criteria will almost certainly simplify the problem of choice and make any judgement-based final decision more reliable.

4

MAKING THE IMPOSSIBLE DECISION

Managers are sometimes faced with making a decision when they have not the faintest idea which way to go. This situation often arises where facts and figures cannot be obtained and gut-feeling is all there is to go on.

It can be argued that managers should avoid the risk of taking action when there is no evidence to guide them but, in real life, such action is sometimes thrust upon them. For example, market research or past experience may suggest that a new product or service will do well in a number of overseas markets. It is important to launch the product in the best market (rather than the worst) of those available. Only one or two markets can be coped with at the outset and the problem is which to choose.

Alternatively, four sites are available for a new factory. The cost is roughly similar and all have roughly equivalent road and rail services. Future governments may axe one of the rail links (or all) and in all cases there is doubt as to whether local authorities will, in future, provide enough public housing to meet the needs of an expanding work force. In other words, the future may depend on the political character of future governments or local councils. Which site should be chosen – or should all be rejected?

In such cases opinions can be divided and opinions can fluctuate. The manager must make a decision. This decision should be supported by his colleagues who should be given the opportunity to participate in the decision-making process.

A way to decide

Since in these 'insoluble' cases the decision must of necessity be based mainly on experience and gut feeling, the more experience/gut feeling which can be brought to bear on the problem the better. The following process is recommended.

1. Select some colleagues to participate in the decision-making process. Ensure they are all briefed on the nature of the problem and have all the information available.

2. List the alternative choices and ask each participant to rank them in descending order of preference. (N.B. This must be done individually and without conferring with colleagues.)

3. Analyse the results and list the top two or three favourite choices.

4. Give each participant this list and ask them to select (privately again) their preference.

5. Take the majority choice resulting from 4 as the decision to be taken.

This technique may be varied according to the number of choices available or other factors. The number of selection runs may be increased giving people more time to think and a greater or lesser number of choices available on the short-list.

Making the impossible decision

The technique avoids the problem of one very dominant individual swamping the instincts of his colleagues by forceful oratory but allows the preferences of colleagues to affect the thinking of each individual. The result tends to be a fair representation of the experience of the group as a whole and is more readily acceptable to all as the best decision under the circumstances. In short, combined wisdom is fairly expressed, giving the enterprising manager a better chance of getting it right.

5

GETTING THE ORGANISATIONAL STRUCTURE RIGHT – NINE ASPECTS TO LOOK AT

There are times when a manager is troubled with a sneaking feeling that the organisational structure is not right but is not quite sure where to look. A sound structure, with all the functions and people effectively allocated to the various jobs to be done will not, alone, ensure an efficient operation. However, a well thought-out structure provides a framework for effective management and is a subject that the manager should pay a lot of attention to. A muddled *unorganised* business will be wasteful of labour, slow to respond to opportunities or threats and will be an unhappy business to work in. A situation which the enterprising manager will find entirely unacceptable!

It is most unlikely that any particular structure will be indefinitely the most suitable. It is easy for a structure to drift out of date and into a muddle. For this reason regular reviews are necessary to ensure that modifications are made to meet changing needs and circumstances. The check-list which follows will give managers a plan of action when reviewing the organisation. The various topics apply in greater or lesser degree whether applied to large or small organisations or to the whole or part of an organisation.

Getting the organisational structure right

1. Is too much loaded on too few?

In the 1950s, management textbooks recommended that the 'span of command' should be limited to five people being supervised by one. Strictly following these numbers can be ignored but the principle is right. When the boss has too many people *requiring his attention regularly* something has to give.

The symptoms of too wide a span of command are:

- Poor-quality work – resulting from insufficient training, help or monitoring.

- Delays – normally due to delayed decisions.

- Poor morale – due to people feeling neglected.

- Lack of forward planning – because the boss has no time for it.

This problem is often found near the top of a company which has grown very rapidly and is often made worse by a failure to delegate. In these situations too much is demanded of too few in the most senior positions.

Delegation (see Chapter 13 for the ways and means) is the solution to the problem, with authority given along with responsibility. It is often necessary to create a new position altogether (perhaps employing a new person from outside) in order that a job which has grown will receive the attention it deserves.

Real life cases which have been observed are:

- The managing director who spent about 50 per cent of his time involving himself in sales and sales management. This meant that he was physically absent too often for the health of a business which had grown to a size where a sales manager was both needed and justified.

- A chief chemist who spent too much time at the laboratory bench and not enough with plant engineers. The routine testing and analysis that the chief chemist spent much of his time on should have been delegated to a junior, enabling him to deal with vital production problems.

- The head of a computer department who was over-occupied with programming and machine-operating. Too little time was spent in forward planning, discussions with users and helping staff. Appointment of and delegation to a chief programmer and senior operator respectively solved this particular problem.

2. Are groups of people too big?

The larger a group of workers becomes the harder it is to maintain a team feeling. Unofficial splinter groups will form, usually along social type lines. Thus, an informal and possibly damaging division may occur between older and younger members of the group and between men and women.

Managers should consider breaking down large groups of, say, 20 people into smaller units of, say, five or six. This can be combined with some degree of specialisation, if appropriate to the work to be done. An additional advantage can be gained by appointing team leaders for the smaller units. This provides promotional opportunities for the more ambitious and able people and creates a source of future managers. Of course, adequate training in supervision must be given to the team leaders before they are given their new responsibilities.

3. Is there any emergency cover?

Cover for unexpected absences (or even planned absences such as holidays) or for a sudden surge of urgent work is an old management problem.

Getting the organisational structure right

The worst effects of unexpected lack of manpower can be minimised by training and delegation but an organisational idea – the 'commando squad' – is worth considering. The squad consists of a small number of people (usually three or four) well trained in a wide range of the skills of business. Members of this squad are moved into departments in difficulties to plug the gap. Sometimes the whole squad is used together to tackle a problem but more frequently they are used singly.

It is important that members of the squad are:

- Adequately paid for the skills required.

- Not allowed to become permanent members of a department – a time limit should be agreed in advance.

- Not under the control of a line manager who will monopolise their services.

- Given an incentive in the form of *real* consideration for a line management job after, say, 1–2 years in the squad, if that is what they prefer.

Some commando squads have been used as a good training ground by placing in them one or two promising youngsters to work alongside the experienced hard core of the squad. Care must be taken to ensure that the power of the squad is not diluted by too many less experienced people but the advantage comes in giving them wide training and exposure to a range of company activities. This can be a good apprenticeship for a more senior position later on.

4. Divisional or functional?

When a business starts it is usually small. The senior people do a bit of everything. The managing director may do the sales planning and the production planning whilst the production manager also handles research and development, maintenance and distribution. As the company expands, specialisation develops resulting in the sales manager handling several products. A production team making a range of goods and central services such as accountants appear working across the products and activities.

Thus, people are split in functional terms – sales, production, accounting, research and so on.

```
              MANAGING
              DIRECTOR
    ┌────────────┼────────────┐
PRODUCTION    SALES      ACCOUNTING
```

The functional structure tends to be centralised and has been found to work best in small businesses or large businesses with a simple product range. It does not work well where the business environment changes frequently, but has the following advantages:

- The managing director is in touch with operations (if he so chooses!).

- It is task-orientated which means that specialists can play a part in management. This has a motivating effect.

- Contact points with outsiders are well defined.

- Lines of command are usually clear and short and the managing director is in a position to resolve internal conflict.

However, this structure also has disadvantages:

Getting the organisational structure right

- It does not respond well to product diversification or market opportunities, e.g. production and sales work in different 'pockets' and tend to see things parochially.

- Profit responsibility rests on one man – the managing director.

- Middle management become parochial, e.g. entrepreneurial action is not encouraged.

- Scope for succession and management development is limited to opportunities arising within the function for which people work.

- The managing director is likely to favour the function from which he came and best understands. He may retain parochial attitudes and even have some antipathy towards functions of which he has no first-hand working experience.

An alternative arrangement worth considering in the growing business is the divisional structure.

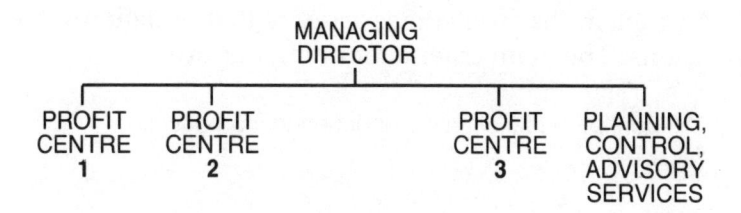

```
                    MANAGING
                    DIRECTOR
    ┌──────┬───────────┴──────┬─────────────┐
  PROFIT  PROFIT           PROFIT        PLANNING,
  CENTRE  CENTRE           CENTRE        CONTROL,
    1       2                3           ADVISORY
                                         SERVICES
```

The divisional structure is appropriate where growth and production diversification have taken place and where profit centres can be clearly seen. It offers the following advantages:

- Profit responsibility is delegated to each profit centre.

- Separate evaluation of the firm's main activities (and products) is easier since those responsible for them are all under one roof.

- Middle management is better motivated as a result of having control over more activities.

- Scope for management development is greater.

- Major decisions are taken nearer the point of action.

- The managing director has time for corporate planning as much of the responsibility is delegated to the profit centres.

- Entrepreneurial action is more likely to emerge.

Each profit centre (division) is a distinct product or geographical sales area *with its own* sales and production operation separate from the other profit centres. With very substantial growth it may be advantageous to develop this even further such that each profit centre has its own separate accounting, research, public relations and other services.

A problem that sometimes arises is that of defining the divisions. The main criteria for doing this are:

- Different products often with independent production facilities.

- Different markets, e.g. different end-users.

- Geography – where cultural differences between markets are important.

- Skills – where specific and differing skills are required to produce and/or sell.

It should also be noted that in some cases conflicts can

Getting the organisational structure right

arise where divisions compete in the same market possibly as a result of over-enthusiasm for subdividing.

5. Is the top too far from the bottom?

'No one ever tells me anything.'
'No one ever knows what is going on.'
'Why do they keep changing their minds?'
'I thought that is what they wanted.'

These expressions heard on the shop-floor can indicate an organisational structure which makes effective communication difficult – both up and down. This is the structure where there is a big boss sitting on top of a string of subordinates reporting one-to-one. In other words there is an 'extended line' structure.

In these structures the clerks, machine operators or whatever, report to a supervisor who reports to the senior supervisor who reports to the assistant general manager who reports to the deputy general manager who reports to the general manager who, finally, reports to the board. Board decisions are passed down through such a long chain that by the time they reach the work force they are out of date and/or distorted. Long chains of commands should be shortened by removing layers – for example by delegation.

6. Who's in charge around here?

It is not unknown to find (a) people reporting to two or more bosses and (b) people reporting to no one at all. The latter often have a boss *in theory* who they never actually see because he is either too busy, never there, or thinks someone else is looking after things.

Enterprising managers should look for any lack of clarity in authority and responsibility for control of work, monitoring of results and feedback to management. While Mr Snooks actively looks after the purchasing section he may not be aware that everyone else expects him to control the general stores. Such gaps in responsibility cover need to be closed.

7. To centralise or to decentralise?

If a management consultant is asked to give his opinion on a centralised function such as filing, accounting, personnel, etc., he will probably recommend decentralisation for the following reasons:

- Decentralised services work more closely with the people they serve and thus serve them better.

- Line managers will use the services more effectively if they have a direct responsibility for them.

- The people concerned get on together better and morale is improved.

The same consultant, finding a decentralised situation, will probably recommend centralisation for the following reasons:

- Centralised services are more economical, i.e. economies of scale can be achieved.

- Centralisation allows more specialisation and thus greater expertise is developed.

- The service can work for the benefit of the business as a whole rather than to please the parochial whims of a line manager.

The management consultant cannot lose because both

Getting the organisational structure right

arguments are valid and, after a change, things will almost certainly improve, for a time at least, due to the 'Hawthorn Effect' – that any change tends to stimulate people and the new arrangement will promote interest in the work.

Managers faced with the centralise/decentralise dilemma will need to examine each of the pros and cons offered and apply some value to them *in the context* of their own business. They might also ask 'are the centralised services'—

- Too powerful? They may be holding up action at the sharp end.

- Too remote geographically?

- Unpopular?

- Growing steadily (and expensively) in numbers.

- Employing ever more numerous specialists in narrow fields.

A positive answer to two or more of the questions suggests decentralisation.

Alternatively, given decentralised services, the following questions might be asked:

- Are there a number of underemployed specialists scattered around?

- Do the line managers really understand the skills (and their application) of these specialists? This particularly applies with computer services. It is not unknown for directors to pay vast sums to external consultants not knowing that their own internal team can do the job perfectly well.

- Would a more effective, economical service result from centralisation?

8. Who talks (and listens) to the outside world?

Every organisation and every part of it needs to be aware of what the outside world (including other departments) believes, expects and wants.

The reviewer should look for *real* communication between functions in the business and *real* communication between the business and the world outside. There should be as a result:

- Coordination between departments. Possibly such coordination should be a specific part of someone's job description.

- Someone listening and talking to: customers; Government departments, institutions and authorities; trade associations; trade unions.

- Someone listening and talking to some of the most important people of all, the employees.

All these functions should be built into the organisational structure.

9. What is going on in the Falklands?

Are there any corners of the organisation which are quietly growing – out of all proportion to needs? Regular candidates for this analysis are:

- Computer departments.
- Filing departments.
- Statistics and records departments.
- Publicity and public relations.

Getting the organisational structure right

- Personnel (central, regional, divisional and area).
- Travel section.
- The Chairman's office (*two* secretaries *and* a P.A.?).
- Accounting departments of all kinds.
- Managers' dining room (close it down!).
- Library services.

Does structure matter in a small department?

Although small departments have the in-built advantage that communications and cooperation are easier – by virtue of having fewer people around – the structure is still important. In particular the manager should strive to ensure that:

(a)   Any function which contributes to and is critical to the objectives and purposes of the department is included in the department. A common example can be found in the provision of computer services to a department from a centralised main-frame facility. The department will inevitably have to take its turn in the various computer runs and will be in competition with other users. Arguments over priorities can arise and, if the computer service fails just as the department's vital weekly run is to be made, the result can be disaster. The departmental manager is often helpless in such situations – or at best must turn to exhausting and expensive manual systems in an attempt to keep his head above water.

The problem can be solved using modern computer technology by placing a small computer *within* the department. Such arrangements may still require an outside service for programming but at least the machine is controlled by the department concerned and there is no dependency on an

[55]

outside agency. Such arrangements often have the advantage of being cheaper. Frequently, since the computer is unlikely to be in use all the time, operating it will be only a part-time activity.

(b) The activities of the department are organised so that any other department being serviced obtains the best possible result. For example, a computer department was responsible for providing a service to about 100 users of word-processors and personal computers in a large office. The programmers, who were also responsible for mainframe systems, were allocated the job of giving a service to the 100 users. This meant constant interruptions to the programmers' other work (which they resented) and unacceptable delays to the small machine users who required a prompt service. To make matters worse the users would telephone any one of the programmers when they were in need of help, there being no one individual allocated to receive messages. The result was delay, frustration, chaos and quite a few lost tempers.

The problem was solved by appointing two programmers to be responsible only for the small machines and by giving them special training. A data control clerk was appointed to receive all telephone calls for help and to allocate the work to the two programmers in an orderly and sensible fashion. The result was a better service, uninterrupted work on main-frame programming and a great deal less aggravation.

(c) Leadership is made entirely clear by avoiding 'deputy to' and 'assistant to' positions. Sometimes such titles are given as a form of promotion or simply to keep happy someone who is worried about status. The result is often confusion over who can make decisions and who should give orders. This in turn causes friction and resentment.

(d) Someone has been clearly designated to stand in for

Getting the organisational structure right

the manager when he or she is absent for lengthy periods. This need can arise for example when a customer service manager is visiting customers over a period of say 2–3 days. The nature of the department's work is such that an immediate response to customers' enquiries will frequently be required and someone must be in a position to make decisions. Naturally, the manager's authority must be delegated along with the manager's responsibility.

6

ARE YOUR STOCK RECORDS REALLY NECESSARY?

I have already mentioned the factory warehouse in Wales in which a card index record of stock was carefully kept. Every movement in and out was faithfully recorded and stock levels re-calculated. In the accounts department another record of the same stock was maintained from copies of delivery and despatch notes. Accounts kept their record because they could not trust the warehouse records. In practice both records were found to be wrong whenever stocktaking was carried out. In such situations the cost of keeping the records is largely a waste. So, is it possible to run the business satisfactorily without keeping stock records at all? In many cases the answer is yes – with time and money saved all round.

Visual stock control

Mr Bloggs who keeps the corner sweet shop does not keep any stock records – he would regard such activity as a waste of his valuable time. When the wholesaler's salesman arrives he glances at the number of cartons on his shelf and mentally calculates whether he needs more stock or not. He knows that he will receive a supply of gob-stoppers about seven days after placing the order and if he has, say, three weeks supply on the shelf, he need not reorder. This means that he will not have too much money unnecessarily tied up in stock or be in danger of failing to supply his customers.

Likewise, if he has an unexpected run on chocolate bars he will note that his shelves are looking empty and telephone the wholesaler for more – without waiting to place his regular order when the representative calls again on his rounds. In effect his stock record is the number of cartons and boxes on his shelves. This is the only stock record which is always correct.

The same principle as Mr Bloggs uses can be applied in a factory (or office stationery store) and is a tried and tested method. ICI Paints Division at Slough were successfully using it over 20 years ago.

How to set up a visual system

Let us take an engineering stores as an example to illustrate what can be done.

The first step is to categorise the stores held into high-value items and low-value items. The high-value items are likely to include a spare motor or two, costly metal items such as platinum crucibles and possibly large stainless-steel machine tools. These items are normally few in number, though representing a high proportion of the stock value. They need no record since it is immediately and visually obvious whether or not they exist and how many of them are in stock.

These high-value items can be placed in a reserved area of the stores with spare motors and the like, being heavy, placed on the floor.

The low-value items (LVIs) will include nuts and bolts, washers, springs, clips, etc., normally supplied in plastic bags or cardboard boxes. These can be arranged on shelves in some convenient way.

The LVI's are the fast movers which generate all the paperwork and for which errors in records are most likely.

It is only too easy to issue a packet of washers and forget to record it. In any case, it takes time and labour to do the recording.

Each LVI requires a simple calculation to determine: (a) minimum stock level and (b) order quantity. Minimum stock level will be the number of washers sufficient to last during the time required to obtain a new delivery. The order quantity will be the amount that should be ordered to benefit from quantity discounts (though not so much that stock levels are unnecessarily too high, too long).

Suppose then that it is decided that the minimum stock of washers is four boxes. These four boxes can be fixed together with a strip of coloured Sellotape which also has an order form attached already made out with the order quantity, code number, etc.

The remainder of the boxes of washers will be stacked alongside the minimum stock – without the sellotape binding. This remaining stock, termed 'free stock', can be issued by the storekeeper as required *without recording anything*. Once the free stock has been used up the storekeeper must break the Sellotape binding to make further issues. This tells him that he must now reorder and he can use the pre-prepared order form to do so. When new supplies arrive he makes up a new minimum stock and prepares a new order form for next time. Thus, the first purpose of a stock record system is met – knowing whether or not it is time to reorder.

The free stock – issued against a requisition as usual but not otherwise recorded – will be constantly reduced to minimum stock level. This, over all the stock items, will tend to reduce stock-holding costs. Dramatic results have been achieved in practice. The vital point is that no new orders are placed until absolutely necessary.

The next requirement of a stock record – telling the accountants the value of the stock for their annual returns – is also easily met. Instead of reading figures from a record card and then trying to reconcile the figures with a stocktaking, the storekeeper merely counts the number of items on the shelf. Stock levels will almost certainly be lower and the job is faster. The minimum stock, obvious because of its Sellotape binding, requires no counting. Adding up the rest is often a case of counting the containers, not the contents.

The details of how to do it must vary from situation to situation and the above described method will need adjustment to suit local circumstances. This does not matter: it is the principle that counts.

Afterthought

If your stock records are kept on a computer the waste of time and level of error may be equally bad, or worse. The computer record is only as good as the information put into it by human beings. In other words, wrong, delayed or both.

One way to minimise the problem – other than switching to a visual system – is to place the computer physically within the stores and wholly under the charge of the storekeeper and his staff. Although some training may be necessary in how to use the machine, this is not difficult with small, modern machines. The stores staff will have *control* of the system. They will thus have an interest in getting the input right and reducing the garbage level in the output. An automatic point-of-sale system can be used when the products being handled are of a suitable type. This will virtually eliminate the problems of incorrect input. It will not of course eliminate a total failure to record a stock movement brought about by by-passing the point-of-sale recording system!

7

CUTTING THE COST
OF COST CONTROL

Many businesses employ people to check invoices received – and, of course, pay them a salary to do it. Obviously no one wants to pay too much as a result of an incorrect invoice but much of the thinking behind present-day controls has its origin in the conditions of thirty or more years ago.

Before the days of machine-prepared invoices and decimalisation, sales clerks hand-drafted invoices involving calculations such as:

>255 Widgets @ £4/3/4½d.
>
>Less 2½% discount.
>
>Plus packaging.

The chance of making a mistake was high and further errors could creep in when a typist copied the hand draft onto an invoice form.

It was necessary in those days to employ a clerk in the accounts or purchasing departments to check each and every invoice to ensure that the arithmetic was correct. It is still necessary today to check quantity billed against a signed delivery note to see that the right number of widgets is being charged for but that is normally a quick and easy task. It is also often a formality since in many cases both of

Cutting the cost of cost control

the documents are prepared simultaneously on a machine, thus guaranteeing identical quantities on each.

Since a machine is almost always used to calculate the cost, the chance of an error of arithmetic is negligible. This gives businesses the opportunity to reduce checking costs and the following process is recommended for doing so.

Step 1

Ask the control clerk (or whoever checks the invoices) to keep a careful record over say, four weeks, of the results of the checking. The information can be recorded under the following headings:

Supplier, Amount invoiced, Error amount, Favourable, Unfavourable

Step 2

At the end of the checking period an analysis can be made of the errors found and the following questions asked:

- Did the total value of errors *in favour of the supplier* exceed the salary cost of the checking procedure?

- Were the errors found mainly in invoices from only one or two suppliers?

Step 3

Depending on what was found in the preceding analysis a number of actions may be decided upon, including:

- Discontinuation of all checking of invoices below, say, £100 in value. This is safer than discontinuing *all* checking and will probably yield the sought-for savings. It is likely that 90 per cent of supply costs will be accounted for by 10 per cent of the invoices (see Chapter 24) and the cost of checking the remaining 90 per cent of invoices is not worthwhile.

- Reporting the results to any 'bad' supplier with regular invoicing errors along with a demand for greater accuracy. Improvements will almost certainly result if the supplier is made aware that a special check on his invoices will inevitably result in slower payment!

- Instituting spot-checks either on all invoices or on certain suppliers only.

The time saved can be spent more productively elsewhere – apart from that the errors in your favour may balance the errors against you!

Studies have shown that more money is likely to be lost by failure to check that invoiced goods have actually been received than by checking the invoices themselves. Did the branch office really receive the 20 boxes of typing paper for which head office has been billed?

Applying the principle elsewhere

The principle that 'the policeman can be more expensive than the thief' can be applied elsewhere. In one situation this was almost literally the case. A factory had a production line which consumed nuts, bolts, washers, springs and other useful and pilferable items. The management, fearing theft of the bits and pieces, had installed a scheme whereby stores staff laboriously counted out the required items and allocated them to the operators on the production line. Records of consumption were kept and everything had to be accounted for at the end of each shift. Naturally the line was held up from time to time when an

Cutting the cost of cost control

operator ran out of supplies and had to wait for his next issue!

The management began to wonder if the controls were really worth it. With some trepidation they decided to scrap them for a time to see what happened. Each production line operator was given large plastic tubs of bits and pieces which the stores staff were told to keep filled up. The records were abandoned and no one had to do any counting up at the end of each shift.

The result was extremely interesting. Consumption in the first week was an all-time record and well in excess of the quantities demanded by the production completed. However, after that, consumption fell to a figure slightly below the old rate.

The conclusion reached by the managers was that some pilfering was inevitable but once any dishonest operator realised that there was no checking he would only take something *when he really wanted it*. He would know that the tub of nuts and bolts was always available. The really important point was that the labour costs saved by removing the controls far outweighed the losses once the first week was over and the system settled down.

Other possible applications for the principle include:

- Checking outgoing invoices to spot undercharging.

- Virtually any other form of routine check that a manager can find. A useful question to ask is 'how often do we find a mistake?'

8

SOLVING COMPLICATED PROBLEMS

Simulation as a technique for solving business problems is gradually gaining acceptance as part of the repertoire of the 'scientific manager'. It is unfortunate that the fullest use of simulation is often not made because of the rather complicated mathematics – and baffling jargon – with which the technique is often associated.

Simulation can be of help when a number of variables interact on each other to result in many alternative conditions. Such a problem occurs when a new product is being planned. Amongst other things management faces the difficulty of determining the overall effect of the new product's varying sales levels on company resources and also on other products competing for those same resources. Similar problems arise in planning labour on a large construction job or in any situation where the effects of bad weather, machinery failures or shortage of transport are difficult to forecast.

The problem is familiar, but in too many cases management is unable or unwilling to make more than guesses when working out forward plans. The complexity caused by the permutation of many factors can appear so great that nothing short of advanced mathematics and a computer can provide the guidance management requires. The manager who cannot call upon these resources is only too often forced into the risky alternative of going ahead and hoping that chance will produce the optimum result.

However, mathematical models can be replaced by 'paper models', which, providing adequate imagination is applied, will give at the very least a good indication of the results of taking various lines of action. Common sense is the only 'special skill' required. The use of such a paper model is best illustrated by a case taken from real life.

Service with economy

The problem arose in a small factory producing a chemical. The production process involved several stages of which two were dominant with regard to total output. The products from the earlier of the two stages (Stage A) could be of six basic types. These were consumed in the later stage (Stage B) to produce many varieties of finished product, each of which required only one of the six basic Stage A types as a raw material.

The nature of the process was such that output from Stage A could only be produced in batches of several tons, while the output of Stage B could be in batches of almost any size. Thus a customer's order for, say, 200 kg of one of the Stage B finished products would call upon a similar quantity from a much larger Stage A batch. Customers' orders were random in nature and could call for any quantity of any of the many products from Stage B.

The situation presented a problem in deciding how to ensure that in-process stocks would be in balance with finished product requirements. It was desirable to avoid the necessity of making a large Stage A batch to satisfy a small Stage B requirement. At the same time production economics demanded that successive Stage A batches should be of the same type for as long as possible.

A certain amount of hopper storage was available for in-process stocks but random customer requirements meant a constant danger that hoppers would become filled with unwanted product. A costly hand-to-mouth situation would result. With customer service a top priority there was no question of delaying production at any stage for convenience.

Three theories were put forward:

1. An extension to the existing clerical procedures would enable a balance to be achieved.

2. No such extension was necessary. Day-to-day 'seat-of-the-pants' working was sufficient and better than the clerical methods.

3. Additional hopper capacity would have to be arranged if balance was to be achieved.

Since the second opinion was too risky to try in practice without further evidence and the third was very costly, it was decided to simulate the first and second methods. The problem to be solved was real and could only be properly simulated using real-life data. The first step was to collect the necessary information.

All the customer orders received in the previous six months were collected and made up into a file in the exact order in which they had been received.

Next, production records for the same period were analysed for machine down-time. Thus real-life records of breakdowns and maintenance were provided. Finally, the precise in-plant situation for a recent day was recorded to show hopper usage, machines under maintenance, raw material stocks, etc., at a particular 'frozen time'.

After these data had been compiled, it was necessary to prepare the simulation rules and to select the appropriate simulation team.

The actual output figures for the various parts of the production process were agreed and listed. Restraints such as sequence of product limitations, labour flexibility, special raw material delivery times, etc., were collected and

Solving complicated problems

agreed with plant personnel. These data were required to ensure that in any given situation which might develop during simulation there would be no doubt as to the unavoidable results or the courses of action which could be taken.

A team of knowledgeable plant personnel was chosen to represent the various activities in the simulation and to make decisions in accordance with the circumstances. Team members included chemists, foremen, a planning clerk, an accountant and an engineer. An umpire was chosen whose function was to issue data, ensure that the rules were adhered to, and to supervise generally.

The team was assembled in a suitable room and supplied with an adequate stock of stationery. Members dealing with particular aspects of the factory management sat together at their own specified tables.

The simulation commenced with a statement provided by the umpire informing each section of the team of the situation in each part of the factory. A few minutes were allowed for members to familiarise themselves with their various material stocks and the state of their equipment. Orders on hand were then issued and examined. All these data were derived from the frozen time mentioned earlier. Further customers' orders were now issued exactly as received in real life for the first simulated day.

The team received such information as they would normally receive in real life from their colleagues and decisions were made in regard to output, schedules, etc. From the records previously analysed the umpire introduced machine breakdowns, delays, labour shortage and any other hold-ups which might occur in real life.

The team members amended and adjusted their plans accordingly within the limitations previously agreed. Production runs arranged by the team were logged against a time scale and the days completed were checked off. Orders were filled as product became available and despatches were logged showing how far customers' delivery dates were met. More new orders were fed in at the appropriate time and a careful note made of any out-of-balance situation or failure.

This process was continued until the team and the umpire were satisfied that the system used had been given a thorough trial. The simulation was later repeated using the alternative system and results compared.

The major factor for measuring success was frequency of completion of customer orders within the lead-time required. However, whenever the team had chosen an expensive way out of a difficult situation the accountant quoted a cost from a table of standards previously prepared and the frequency of each case of high-cost expedient was then taken into consideration.

The simulation showed that extra hoppers were not necessary but that an extension to the clerical system *was* required for acceptable results. The frequency of high-cost expedients was roughly equal in both cases.

The company's management gained two advantages:

1. Conclusive evidence clearly supporting the use of a particular system where previously the matter was considerably in doubt.

2. A practical demonstration of the superiority of the better system to the personnel who ran the plant. This caused the staff to have confidence in the chosen system, especially since those who originally opposed it had been given an opportunity to prove it as drastically as common sense (and the umpire) would allow.

Simulation of this type can take anything from an hour to two or three days depending on how much real time requires simulation. However, quite frequently the weaknesses in a system will emerge within the first hour.

Here are a few additional points to bear in mind in preparing a simulation exercise:

- The utmost care should be taken to avoid simplifying the problem to make it easier to simulate. One of the advantages of simulation is its tendency to show up apparently trivial factors as critical. Leaving out some of the smaller points can give rise to misleading results.

- The real-life situation must be faithfully copied. Preparation should preferably involve only real-life data to be applied to the game in a real-life way by the participants.

- A firm and intelligent umpire is essential. The umpire must ensure that team members only make decisions which are feasible and also that members do not acquire information that in real life would be denied them.

- Lastly, all the team members must fully understand the purpose of the simulation, the system under test and the absolute necessity of being completely honest.

Some tips on evaluating the results

Frequently, as in the example given in this chapter, the results of the simulation become readily obvious to the participants and evaluation is easy. Sometimes, however, there is doubt as to the validity of the results which can be cleared up in one of the following ways:

- Testing the apparent conclusion by repeating the simulation using specially 'cooked-up' data designed to push the system to its limits.

- Repeating the original simulation using a team of informed but *independent* people.

- Using the original data to carry out a second simulation under the new system indicated by the first run.

IDEAS FOR ENTERPRISING MANAGERS

In most cases the last option is the most helpful in reducing the chances of drawing the wrong conclusions. Repeating the exercise in any manner may appear tedious but it is certainly better than trying it out in the factory and finding that things are worse than before!

9

THE PRICE OF MEETINGS

Surveys show that many managers spend a substantial amount of their time listening and talking and that much of this takes place in meetings. Many of these get-togethers (sometimes termed 'conferences' when attended by the more august people in the organisation) are of a regular and routine type. All or some of the following will be familiar to most managers:

- Sales review meeting.
- Quality control committee.
- Works liaison committee.
- Budget review.
- Production planning group.
- Cost reduction teams.
- Employee relations committee.
- Social committee meeting.
- Canteen committee.
- Annual management conference.

- Financial review team.

- Development study group.

- Public relations committee.

- Office administration meeting.

and so on, and so on, and so on.

There are also a number of external meetings which managers may attend – usually termed seminars. These are often of the one-day variety and organised by a commercial body that provides a lecturer on a particular subject and charges a fee to hear him. The term 'conference' is also used in the case of the more up-market of these gatherings. Use of the term often means that a politician will be giving an introduction, a lunch-time address or making the closing remarks. If we add to all this the internal ad hoc meetings and the external symposia, colloquia and discussion groups there is a potentially huge demand on the time of managers.

The O & M analyst presented with the problem of an over-extended manager would invariably find out how much of his time was taken up with meetings and try to assess their purpose and value. Having done so the really difficult job was to convince the manager (or his boss) that either a particular meeting was largely a waste of time or the attendance of the manager concerned was unnecessary. The trick, which the enterprising manager can use to his advantage, is to quote the cash cost of the meetings.

Arguing that a meeting achieves little or nothing is not likely to gain very much. Those who attend it, particularly the chairperson, will be reluctant to agree that they have been wasting their time. Apart from that there may be some status aspect to chairing or attending a meeting which will be defended on the grounds that the meetings *do* achieve something. However, placing the cash cost in front of the

The price of meetings

people concerned has a markedly sobering effect and, experience shows, prompts a re-think of the situation.

The following table (which can be used as a ready reckoner) shows the costs which can be attributed to meetings. The figures are based on a seven-hour day and a working year of 234 days.

COST OF TIME SPENT

Salary p.a.	1 minute	10 minutes	1 hour
£ 5,000	5p	50p	£ 3.00
£10,000	10p	£1.00	£ 6.00
£15,000	15p	£1.50	£ 9.00
£20,000	20p	£2.00	£12.00
£25,000	25p	£2.50	£15.00

So if five managers at an average salary around £15,000 spend 10 minutes discussing something the cost to the company will be about £7.50. If, say, eight more senior managers at £25.000 p.a. each spend a day in discussion the cost will be around £840.

Enterprising managers involved in a do-it-yourself analysis will ask the following questions:

- Does the meeting under review produce results clearly worth the cost?

- Could any visible results of the meeting have been achieved in another, less expensive way?

- How many future meetings can be cut out – and how much money could be saved?

- What is the saving worth in terms of gross sales figures? For example, if £5,000 p.a. is saved this is worth about £50,000 sales revenue when gross profit is about 10 per cent.

IDEAS FOR ENTERPRISING MANAGERS

It is clearly easier to save the £5,000 than to make an extra sale of £50,000.

This is not intended as an argument against having *any* meetings – some will be essential in order that joint decisions can be made. Indeed, in an earlier chapter the use of meetings has been recommended as a way to improve communications. However, meetings should be looked at from time to time to see how necessary or useful they really are. Knowing the cost can put things in a clearer perspective.

If it is decided that a particular routine meeting is worth its cost, it obviously pays to ensure that the meeting is efficiently conducted. A useful source of advice on this topic is the film 'Meetings, Bloody Meetings' produced by Video Arts Ltd. and featuring John Cleese and Timothy West.

Video Arts also produce a companion booklet to the film called *How to run a meeting*. This booklet, written by Anthony Jay, includes in its 31 pages advice on:

- The function of a meeting.

- Frequency and composition of meetings.

- Preparing for a meeting, e.g. defining the objectives.

- The chairman's job.

- Conducting the meeting.

- Controlling the participants.

- Follow-up.

Part 2

The People Asset

Neglecting the people in the company is at least as bad as not maintaining machinery or failing to invoice the customers. A well-trained, happy and enthusiastic team is a major asset for every enterprising manager and well worth spending time and effort to achieve.

Much of Part 2 is devoted to aspects of training – a matter only too often neglected despite the fact that performance is heavily dependent on job knowledge and job skill. The enterprising manager will want his staff to be properly trained so that they will not only work productively but will be motivated and happy as well. Enterprising managers will want enterprising staff to work with.

Part 2

The People Asset

10

STAFF SELECTION

The involvement of managers in the selection of their staff varies from organisation to organisation. Some organisations take the view that staff selection is not part of a manager's duties and leave this task to a central service department such as Personnel. However, there are a number of arguments which strongly favour the manager's involvement and the enterprising manager will be keen to take part for the following reasons:

- The manager must work closely with all his staff, and must develop a close relationship with them in order to produce results. Therefore he should have some say about who should join his team.

- The manager knows the work and is aware of the personal qualities and technical skills required to do the job. Therefore, he should be well able to assess the capability of the applicant for the job.

However, many managers find staff selection difficult and may need to rely too heavily on others such as the Personnel Department. The following is a process which, if followed, will make the task for the manager reasonably easy.

IDEAS FOR ENTERPRISING MANAGERS

1. Preparation

Start with a clear definition of what is wanted. This definition will include a detailed job description and a person profile.

The job description will include the following items as a minimum. In some cases it will be necessary to look ahead to see how the job might develop and to include any development expectations in the description as well.

- Job title.

- Function.

- Tasks, duties, responsibilities.

- Location of job.

- To whom reporting.

From this description the person profile describing the required personal qualities, technical skills, etc., can be extracted. Without the job description there is a tendency to miss out some of the necessary requirements.

The 'culture' of the department should also be taken into account when deciding what age and personality type would most readily fit in. The social compatibility of newcomers with an established group is important in maintaining a harmonious and cooperative environment. The profile of the ideal person will allow for this factor.

Person profiles will, of course, vary according to the nature and demands of the work to be done. Considerable thought may be required in preparing the profile. Even if the needs of the job are well understood much care should be taken in writing the person profile for it. There are two helpful tips in profile writing, viz.:

- Never assume that the person best suited for a vacancy

Staff selection

should be similar to the outgoing incumbent. The departure of someone from a job is an opportunity to reassess the nature of the job and how it should be done. It should be borne in mind that the way the job has been done in the past will have been influenced by the skills and other attributes of the person doing it.

A common situation to be found in the 1980s is work carried out manually which has remained a manual operation only because the employee concerned was not computer literate. If the profile of the new recruit includes either computer skills or the ability to be trained to use a computer, an opportunity to improve efficiency can be taken.

- When preparing the profile each attribute of the person required should be matched with a short 'reason why' statement. This discipline encourages objective thinking and helps to avoid making such mistakes as asking for levels of education which are not necessary. One manager who suffered continuous high turnover in staff made the mistake of insisting on employing only young university graduates – for jobs which such people found undemanding, boring and with no future.

A typical person profile may look like this:

Person Profile for Senior Sales Liaison Clerk

Attribute   *Reason*

1. **Age range: 25 to about 45 yrs.**

   Some maturity needed to deal with sales staff and customers and to supervise office juniors. The upper age limit is likely to be influenced by ability to work with IBM personal computers.

2. **Experience.**

   Minimum 2 years in chemicals sales office.

   Knowledge of technical terms necessary.

IDEAS FOR ENTERPRISING MANAGERS

Minimum 4 years in sales support.	Understanding of sales environment and ability to identify urgent/priority situations.
Use of IBM small computers.	Sales forecast compilation.
Supervision of junior clerks.	Leadership of stocks and production section.

3. Formal education.

'O' levels English and mathematics.	Preparation of stock and progress reports, including statistical analysis.

4. Personality.

Calm and self-contained.	To deal with pressure from sales force.
Diplomatic, courteous.	Dealing with customers and transport contractors.
Firm and tenacious.	Pressures, e.g. in stock shortage situation and dangers of taking undesirable expediency action.
Ability to learn exporting routines.	To meet possible move into freight forwarding and/or direct exports.

5. General.

Ambitions satisfied with existing level of authority and responsibility.	No prospect of significant promotion.
A good anchor-man.	Continuity and maintenance of standards in the office.

The above profile is of course purely an example to show the type of personal attributes which may be included and the way in which the profile can be laid out. With more

Staff selection

senior or demanding jobs the ideal attributes may need to be described in greater detail.

It should be remembered that the profile as written is describing the ideal person. Such people are difficult to find and it is likely that a 'best fit' candidate will, in most cases, be chosen. This should not be regarded as a disaster and any significant variation from the ideal can often be catered for by some adjustment to the working arrangements. It may, for example, be possible to reallocate work between the various people so that any lack of experience or skill in the new recruit can be covered by one of the existing staff. This could be a temporary arrangement while the recruit is given appropriate training or a permanent *exchange* of work. Care must be taken, however, to ensure that there is no real or imagined additional burden placed on existing staff to compensate for any shortcomings in the recruit.

2. Consultation

Having completed the job description and person profile the manager should have sufficient information with which to go to the Personnel Department for advice and help in recruitment. A full discussion should be held on the type of candidate required and, if necessary, the person profile amended to take account of any new ideas or conclusions which have emerged as a result.

3. Interview

At some later stage interviews will take place. The purpose of the interview is to gather information about the interviewee. The manager can then compare this information with the original requirements which were drawn up in the preparation stage, and on the basis of this comparison, make a decision.

IDEAS FOR ENTERPRISING MANAGERS

The use of the following checklist will be helpful in the interview process:

INTERVIEW CHECKLIST

(a) Before the interview – look at the following questions.

- Has the interviewee been told the time and purpose of the interview?

- Has all the relevant available information about the job and the interviewee been obtained and studied?

- How shall I open the interview?

- What specific points should be dealt with?

- What questions may the interviewee ask?

- Have I got all the facts such as pension scheme details, holiday entitlement, salary, working hours, locations, etc.?

- Is the environment right? For example:

- Is the interview area private?

- Is the seating arranged comfortably and in such a way that neither person is at a disadvantage?

- Can I ensure that interruptions will not occur, or at least be kept to an unavoidable minimum?

(b) The interview itself

The most important thing about the interview is that it is a means of getting information. The information is obtained

Staff selection

from the *answers* that the interviewee gives to questions or volunteers. The interviewer must, therefore, encourage the interviewee to talk as much as possible; his own contribution must be concerned with providing the right sort of atmosphere in which the interviewee will talk freely about himself.

Research has shown that almost everybody enjoys talking about themselves – the interviewer therefore has only to provide the opportunity.

The following are the important points to be borne in mind whilst conducting the interview:

- Put the interviewee at ease. Smile and be friendly.

- Explain the purpose of the interview. It is not an inquisition, but a meeting to achieve a mutually beneficial result.

- Encourage the interviewee to talk – ask questions which demand more than a yes/no answer. Make encouraging noises. Nod in agreement.

- Keep your own talking to a mininum.

- Be attentive to what the interviewee says – and to what is not said.

- Subordinate your own feelings. For example, if the interviewee says something that irritates you do not attack him or drop your friendly manner. Any such response is likely to cause the interviewee to retreat into a shell or become emotional.

- Watch your control of the interview – are you getting the information you want? Asking a question can bring the discussion round to the subject you are interested in.

- Avoid boasting about your importance, aggressive questions, irrelevant questions and overselling the company or job.

(c) After the interview

Having conducted the interview, it is important that time is given to analysing and reflecting on what has happened. What information did you get? What impression have you formed of the interviewee? What about your own performance? Were there any weaknesses in your technique that you are aware of? If so, what can be done to avoid them in future?

Consider the following points:

- How well did the candidate fit the requirements for the job?

- How important are the items where fit was not very close?

- Is the candidate so strong on some points that they more than balance the weak points?

- Can the job itself be slightly altered to fit an otherwise good candidate? What effect would the changes have on existing staff?

- Were any important aspects missed or skimped? Is a second interview (perhaps with a colleague) worthwhile?

- Will the candidate's personality fit in with other staff?

- Do the candidate's ambitions fit in with the job? For example, a very ambitious high flyer will not long be content with a dull job with little future. On the other hand, a demanding job often requires an ambitious person

- Have I allowed my prejudices (we all have them!) to influence my judgment – either way?

As with many skills, practice makes perfect. If the above checklists are used, the manager will find staff selection an interesting and potentially rewarding activity which he can **perfectly well do himself.**

11

MAKING APPRAISAL SCHEMES WORK

Appraisal schemes have in recent years fallen out of favour in many organisations. This has resulted from the frequent failure of such schemes, often for reasons which could well be avoided. Careful handling makes a potentially very valuable technique a practical proposition. The reasons for failure fall into one or more categories.

- The result of the appraisal interview is used to determine salary awards.

  Linking money with appraisal will inevitably be disastrous as the appraisee will never readily accept that he has weak areas. One of the main purposes of appraisal is to identify areas for improvement and agree on what is needed to achieve the improvement. If the appraisee fears a loss of income it is not unreasonable that he will fight to the death in resisting criticism. All objectivity will disappear.

- Managers find appraisal interviews with unsatisfactory employees uncomfortable and embarrassing and will consequently postpone them indefinitely.

  There should be a central control from, say, the Personnel Department to ensure that the interviews take place. Managers must also realise that handling the difficult cases is a prime role of management. The difficult case can be potentially the most rewarding for the manager, employee and the company.

- Managers are not given any guidance or training as to how to conduct the appraisal interviews (sometimes they are unaware of the purpose) and appraisees are not always aware that the appraisal scheme is, or should be, in their interest.

Assuming that the organisation as a whole resolves the first two problems the following is a checklist to aid the enterprising manager in dealing with the last:

What is an appraisal interview?

The appraisal or staff development interview is the means by which the manager and subordinate come together to discuss the subordinate's performance and its relationship to the work of the department over a given time. The manager gives his impression of the appraisee's performance to the appraisee. This is discussed with a view to establishing an objective evaluation of the appraisee's past performance *which is acceptable to both parties* and a clearly understood and agreed set of objectives, performance standards and targets for the future.

The purposes of this process are:

- To develop and motivate individuals in their present jobs and for any intended future assignments.

- To let individuals know where they stand and what the manager thinks of their work.

- To help individuals to understand how they can improve themselves and also to identify how the company can help them, for example by providing training.

- To recognise good work – and let the appraisee know this.

Making appraisal schemes work

- To assess the work of the department as a whole. This gives the manager an insight into morale and 'feeling' in the department – and any action which should be taken to correct deficiencies.

- To give the appraisee an opportunity to freely express aspirations, fears, dissatisfactions, preferences, etc.

If the interview is to contribute to the company's policy on manpower planning and development, the manager must be aware of, and keep in mind when preparing for the interview:

- Possible career patterns (i.e. those affected by company long-term policy).

- Organisational changes likely in the future which may have an influence on the appraisee's career or work.

Preparation

It is important to prepare fully and carefully for the interview and the manager should include the following:

- Advice to the appraisee of the time and place of the interview – and an explanation of the purpose of the interview. Confirmation that the purpose is truly understood and that no irrational fears are lurking about in the appraisee's mind is an essential requirement.

One very successful company gives each employee the following *written* statement as *part* of the process of ensuring that the purposes of the appraisal scheme are fully understood:

> 'One of the major goals of the firm is to enable each of its members to achieve the highest possible level of performance. The realisation of this goal is essential to the provision of a first-class service to clients and to the

continuing success of our firm. It is equally a goal to which we believe each individual member of the firm aspires, at whatever stage of his or her career, since the opportunity to contribute to the best of our ability is a need common to all of us.

The achievement of a high level of performance is to a very large extent dependent on the following conditions:

> clear understanding of the results expected of you at any stage of your career with the firm
>
> regular review of your work so that your actual level of performance can be compared with the results expected
>
> periodic evaluation of your progress to establish what you do well and in which areas improvement is needed
>
> appropriate guidance and training to help you build on your strengths and overcome any significant weaknesses
>
> planning of your development in such a way that your career is able to progress in the most constructive direction
>
> due recognition of the contribution that you are making.'

This company also uses, as part of an on-going assessment system, reports on performance including a provision for the employee to comment on his or her performance. Once again the reason is explained to the employees as follows:

> 'The objective of incorporating into performance reports a requirement for you to comment on your own progress is to encourage you to evaluate how the work that you were allocated has contributed to your development and in which aspects of performance you believe you

Making appraisal schemes work

have done well or need to improve. There is often a tendency to be reticent about what you see as your strengths and weaknesses but to a considerable extent your development depends on your own acknowledgement of areas in which additional experience or training would be of benefit and you should be prepared to discuss these matters with the person reporting on your work so that appropriate further action can be arranged.'

- An allowance of adequate and *uninterrupted* time for the interview.

- Familiarisation with all the details of the person and his job.

- Certainty about the purpose of the interview itself.

- Consideration of his own attitudes towards the appraisee. The manager must be objective and not allow any personal feelings about the employee to cloud his judgement.

- Some ideas for future development, help or training which would suit the individual appraisee.

Conducting the interview

- Open with a few neutral remarks to enable both parties to settle down.

- Discuss achievements or failures specifically. Generalisations should be avoided as they can give rise to a sense of unfairness *and* are difficult to deal with.

- Use open questions to obtain more expression of feelings, attitudes and motives. Questions demanding yes or no answers result in very little to go on.

- Listen to what is said – don't interrupt. The appraisee will be encouraged to talk more freely if facing a willing listener.

- Don't become emotionally involved by defending yourself or showing annoyance. A neutral technique should be employed throughout.

- Put yourself in the appraisee's place and see the situation from his point of view.

- Try to work for agreement for the future – avoiding overlong inquests on past problems.

- Give opportunities for the appraisee to ask questions and make comments. Suggestions for future action should be encouraged.

- Review the points you have discussed and agreed on.

- Note the points where action has to be taken.

- Focus on building for the future.

Above all, the appraisal interview should be free, frank and friendly. Appraisees should be able to put forward their own ideas and opinions (even if unpalatable) without fear or favour. Without this frankness much of the potential benefit can be lost.

The result of the interview

At the end of the interview there should be an agreed plan of action (however simple or limited) designed to help the appraisee with difficulties and to make the most of the appraisee's abilities. The plan should, as far as is humanly possible, match both the appraisee's ambitions for the future and the company's forward plans.

A written list of things to be done, both by appraisee and manager, should be included in the plan. For example:

Appraisal action plan

Manager	Employee	Purpose
1. Arrange for day release to local college.	Attend course on basic statistics.	To overcome difficulties in dealing with production reports.
2. Discuss work problems with section leader.		To remove apparent grievances.
3.	Increase contact with production departments.	To improve understanding of production problems and improve cooperation.

Short-term follow-up

The end of the interview is not the end of the task. The manager must follow up at appropriate intervals and keep in touch to ensure that the agreed plan is being followed. Too often the appraisal action plan degenerates into a list of good intentions which are never carried out. Should this occur then valuable time has been wasted and, even worse, the appraisee has been let down. It is not unknown for appraisees, looking forward to promised help or experience opportunity, to feel bitter and betrayed when nothing happens. The manager in such cases will have a demotivated, possibly hostile, employee on his hands instead of a motivated and supportive employee who will be an asset to him in future. A future asset is what the appraisal should be aiming for.

Looking further ahead

One of the benefits to be gained from the appraisal system is the opportunity to assess the future potential of the employee in addition to achieving improvements in the present job. The day-to-day pressures of any manager's job make it difficult to take stock of the potential of individual employees. The appraisal interview – and the thinking that precedes and follows it – gives such an opportunity. Managers should make full use of this by making a conscious effort to consider the clues which will indicate whether or not an employee is capable of greater things. Indications that someone may have potential which can be developed are:

- An expressed desire for more responsibility.

- A history of using initiative and voluntarily taking on tasks which needed to be done.

- Demonstrated ability and willingness to learn – including voluntary action taken to improve knowledge and skills.

- Popularity and influence which might indicate natural leadership skills.

- A constructive and logical approach to problems and their solution.

- Enthusiasm and energy – even when the work is of a dull or routine nature.

- Consistent success – indicating that the individual may not yet be fully stretched.

A 'yes' answer to all or some of the above clues strongly suggests an employee with potential for greater things. It is in the interests of the manager and the company to recognise and use this potential. Good people know, more often than not, that they are good. They will look for their opportunities elsewhere if the present employer is unable or unwilling to give them a future appropriate to their ability.

Managers should not hesitate to provide opportunities for people with potential including recommending them for more demanding jobs in other departments. The temptation to hang on to valued staff should be resisted as a counterproductive exercise. It is far better to keep them in the company – even if not in the department.

Further reading

A booklet published by Video Arts Ltd, *How am I doing*, is a worthwhile read for managers wanting to look further at the appraisal system. Equally helpful is the Video Arts film of the same title. A useful tip is to show the film and/or provide the book to the staff to be appraised as well as the managers who will do the appraising. This will ensure that *everyone* knows what it is all about.

12

TRAINING – SELLING THE IDEA

Most managers like the *idea* of training but very few want to pay for it. The enterprising manager who is keen on training and wants to encourage his seniors and colleagues to adopt a training programme comes up against the cost/benefit problem. It is easy to work out the cost but next to impossible to put a value on the results.

The following check-list is intended to provide the enterprising manager with an argument to convince the opposition. It is based on the benefits of training both to employees and to the company or department.

1. Benefits for the employees

- Training improves confidence and reduces worry and stress. These are very real problems for the employee not sure about what he or she is doing and they can be seriously underestimated by managers who may have forgotten their own times of struggle with an unfamiliar task.

- Job satisfaction is improved by training. Nothing beats the thrill of getting it right and knowing it's right.

- Improved prospects for promotion can result from training. This can be a big motivator for the ambitious junior.

Training – selling the idea

- Even if promotion is not achieved, standing and pay can be improved via training.

- Training means that somebody cares. Too many people go through their working lives feeling that nobody gives a damn about them or what they do.

Some managers, unfortunately, will not be sufficiently interested in their employees to find the above arguments sufficiently convincing. It may be necessary to go on and point out the advantages to the company or department – and indeed to the boss himself. These advantages include the following:

- Training results in better quality work. This can have a bearing on sales, profits and the reputation of the boss.

- Costs are reduced. Fewer errors arise and less wastage results from the work of well-trained people. Correcting errors is an expensive and time-consuming activity.

- Staff turnover is reduced by training and thus recruitment costs are reduced. Not everyone will understand this point but surveys have shown that many new employees leave during the first few weeks or months because they are fed up with not knowing how to do the job properly and the worry that this can cause. The degree of worry can be quite high and is not always fully appreciated by the old hands to whom the work has become second nature.

- When everyone knows what to do and how to do it there are fewer rows and disagreements – all of which waste time and energy and give the trouble makers a golden opportunity.

- When an employee understands what it is all about, initiative is improved. For example, if a clerk is not sufficiently trained to be able to recognise an error he will let it go, like the clerk who mailed an important contract to Nairobi, Nigeria!

- Training makes new employees effective sooner, reducing the expensive learning curve stage.

- Well-trained people turn out more work and thereby reduce labour costs and staff shortage problems.

- Well-trained people enhance the company reputation in a variety of ways. If in doubt, think how you react when you are greeted by a tired, bored, rude receptionist or receive yet another incorrect invoice or statement.

These then are some of the arguments in favour of training which the enterprising manager should be aware of and can use to argue the case for expenditure on training.

13

SETTING UP ON-JOB TRAINING

On-job training is the term used to describe a method by which people learn their jobs in the workplace rather than in a training centre or school. On-job training (OJT) has distinct advantages over classroom courses, of which the following are the most significant:

- OJT is the method which has the least adverse effect on the flow of the work of a department. In other words, training goes on while the work goes on and the trainee can often contribute to output whilst learning.

- Where the trainee is a new employee, he or she can, through OJT, contribute something to the productivity of the department relatively soon after having joined the company – sometimes from the first hour or so.

- Training can be carried out by the supervisor in charge rather than an elusive training officer who may not have enough detailed knowledge of the work. There are tricks of the trade, or knowledge of the peculiarities of certain customers, which the supervisor will be aware of and can include in the training. The result is often a range of skills which are of more immediate practical value than the more theoretical classroom learning.

It is, however, one of the most neglected training methods because of the constraints on the trainer in terms of the time and resources he or she has available. However, if carefully planned, OJT need not be too demanding of time.

The enterprising manager will also find that OJT is easier to get going as he can organise it himself. He can also ensure that the knowledge given to the trainee is exactly what he wants them to be given. In other words *he* is in control.

A planned approach to on-job training

All training must be systematic and carefully planned if it is to be effective, but it is particularly important to plan OJT in advance if the best use of time and resources is to be achieved. It is not good enough, as often happens, for a new employee to be dumped 'next to Nelly' in the pious hope that Nelly will adequately teach the newcomer. The chances are that Nelly will be untrained in the skills of teaching and will do the job badly or, even worse, will teach the trainee the wrong way to do things.

The training plan should consist of the following:

- Finding out *what* the trainee has to be taught in order to learn the job – this is the *assessment of training needs*.

- Setting up a control on the training – *setting objectives* for the trainer and the trainee.

- Collecting all the necessary materials together, working out a time-table, etc. – *preparation and design*.

- The teaching itself – *implementation*.

- Assessing progress, noting problems, difficulties or shortfalls – *evaluation*.

- Where necessary, making alterations – *modification*.

Setting up on-job training

1. Assessing training needs

Examine the job in broad terms noting all the main features such as clerical tasks, manual skills, communication requirements, etc.

Write down a description of the job, stating the following:

- Title of job.

- Purpose of job.

- Job elements, i.e. the things to be done.

- Knowledge required for each element.

- Skills required for each element.

The knowledge and skills defined in the description of the job can be converted into objectives which will help to keep both the trainer and the trainee on the right track when the teaching begins. Objectives should be stated in the following fashion (i.e. never vague):

'Objective: at the end of the training the trainee will be able to complete job sheets and cost sheets and prepare a quotation analysis. The trainee will be able to re-work a quotation analysis from information given in a sales report.'

Note. It is most important that describing the objectives is done thoroughly in order to ensure that:

- The most appropriate things are taught and irrelevant matters are excluded.

- The instructor and trainee have a clear goal to aim at and the instructor knows what examples or other teaching aids are needed.

- Teaching follows a logical sequence.

All this follows from thoughtfully preparing a job description. Many people do not bother with job descriptions as they feel that they know instinctively what the job entails. This is very commonly a mistake realised as soon as a job description is attempted. The discipline of sitting down and writing out the details, especially the knowledge and skills required, can be an eye-opener. The discovery that there is more in the job than appears at first sight is always a likely result of a methodical examination of the job for description purposes.

Collect information about the trainees, e.g. by means of informal interviews. This stage will concentrate on assessing the trainees' present levels of knowledge and abilities but should also be used to gain a feel for the trainees' personalities and general attitudes.

Match the information concerning trainees' current skills and knowledge with the information about the skills and knowledge required to do the job. The difference between the two will be the basis of the training plan.

If, as described in Chapter 11, an appraisal system is used, then much of the training needs of the individuals will be known. The appraisal will also have checked the job description and resulted in knowing the employee's own opinion of weaknesses to be corrected and strengths to be exploited. It may only be necessary to examine some of the detail of the work to be done to go direct from the appraisal to designing the training plan.

2. Designing the plan

Collect together all the information from:

- The job description.
- The needs assessment.

Setting up on-job training

- The objectives.

- The assessment of the trainees. (Possibly resulting from an appraisal interview.)

Break down the training material into:

- Its logical order

  then

- Units of instruction, i.e. teaching sessions.

The size of the units of instruction will be affected by:

- The complexity of the subject. More complex subjects may need to be dealt with in shorter sessions to avoid exhausting or discouraging the trainee. Less complex subjects can be dealt with at greater length.

- The age of the trainee, and your assessment of his/her intelligence, aptitude, personality and ability to learn.

- The physical conditions under which training is to be carried out. For example, sessions should be short if held in noisy workshops or where distractions or interruptions are likely – such as in a retail shop or other place open to the public.

Draw up a timetable based on:

- The number of training sessions required.

- The speed with which the trainee must become effective.

- The time that the trainer has available.

- The resources of the section or department in terms of delegating the training and/or other work.

IDEAS FOR ENTERPRISING MANAGERS

The problem of time

How can the supervisor find the time to train effectively? It is first necessary to accept these facts:

- On-job training requires only short periods of teaching at a time, e.g. 20 minutes.

- Such time *can* be found. In fact supervisors and managers spend such periods at meetings, discussions and social chit-chat in the normal working day.

- Delegation of work can help. The supervisor can hand over his or her work to a second-in-command during the training session.

The process of allocating time is as follows:

- Estimate the *total* time required to teach the trainee the subject (say five hours).

- Estimate the necessary date by which you consider the trainee should know the subject (say three weeks hence).

- Calculate how much time per day is needed to devote to the trainee, on average: 3 weeks = 15 working days; 5 hours' teaching over 15 working days = 20 minutes per day.

- Choose a time each day when the trainer will set aside 20 minutes.

- *Fix* this time as the training time and stick to it. Arrange for someone else to deal with the telephone or other demands and make sure the boss and everyone else knows of and supports the arrangement. If the training session is not regarded as sacrosanct it will be interrupted or disappear altogether.

Setting up on-job training

3. Implementation

Training is a **two-way** process of communication between the trainer and the trainee. Effective instruction will take full account of how people learn and what the trainee needs from the trainer in order to make progress. Therefore, in teaching, the following should be taken into account:

- The trainee's motivation to learn. The benefits to the employee should be pointed out, e.g. any cash advantages.

- Information is best absorbed by demonstration, e.g. filling in a real form is more instructive than merely telling the trainee how one should be filled in. The real-life example is also likely to reveal the oddities and exceptions which crop up from time to time and which tend to be overlooked in theoretical training.

- Information is more easily absorbed and retained when it has a logical structure. In other words, the training should start at the beginning of a process and flow systematically to the end.

- Information is more easily absorbed and retained when one piece of information is linked to another, i.e. the relationship between one task and another should be explained.

- The *whole* job or operation should be explained or demonstrated; then each part; then the whole task repeated. This process makes the whole purpose clear and reinforces learning.

Making the learning and teaching easier

Managers sometimes despair at the apparent inability of their staff to learn. So also do school teachers, university lecturers and training course leaders so there is no reason for the manager or supervisor to feel inadequate as a trainer.

The problem can be reduced to a minumum (and sometimes removed altogether) by taking note, before the teaching session, of those factors which discourage learning and those which encourage it.

The discouraging factors

(a) The material is set at too high a level

It is easy to forget how confusing a subject may be to a beginner. The point has already been made that the experienced old hand may treat a subject as second nature and this can result in the mistake of pitching the instruction at too high a level.

The teaching should be kept at a simple level with material geared to the trainee's – not the instructor's – level of understanding.

(b) The teaching is too fast

Once a trainee has been left behind he or she is lost. Instruction, in easy stages, should in this respect also be designed to suit the trainee, not the instructor.

It is useful to check progress by gentle question sessions to make sure the trainee is keeping up with the work. Not all trainees will say that they have lost the thread. Regular checks will avoid wasted time and a dispirited pupil.

(c) Distractions

In addition to the obvious problems of noise or interruptions, the instructor should remember that discomfort is a major distraction. Hard, uncomfortable chairs and a hot (or

Setting up on-job training

cold) room are examples of conditions which will distract. Everything possible must be done to avoid them. If distractions are unavoidable, allowances for them should be made in the time allocated for the training programme, i.e. learning will be slower in bad conditions so a longer overall period may be necessary.

(d) Lack of examples

The saying that 'a picture is worth a thousand words' is true. People learn more quickly and easily from demonstrations, pictures, films and plenty of real-life examples of how to do it.

(e) Fatigue

Sessions should be kept short with ample breaks for mental and physical relaxation. Trainees should be allowed a break *before* they fall asleep or drop to the floor.

(f) Boredom

This can result from any of the items mentioned so far. It can also result from a weary instructor who drones on and on in the same dull monotone. A bored instructor can cause the trainees to be bored too. The teacher must himself be lively and enthusiastic.

(g) Fear

Instructors must not shout, bully or threaten. A big stick causes fear and fear causes the mind to go into panic mode with the result that thinking and memory become disorganised.

(h) Irrelevant material

Whether or not material is actually irrelevant, if the trainee believes it to be so he will switch off. Instructors should explain the relevance if it is not *absolutely* clear.

(i) Apathy

Check that the trainee knows why he or she is there. If there seems to be no point in the training or no apparent advantages to be gained from it the trainee will lose interest – or even start with no interest.

(j) Jargon

The jargon of the trade will be familiar to the instructor but not to the trainee. It should be explained – including those items referred to by initials or code numbers. In other words, make sure that the trainee knows that R & D stands for Research and Development or that DP stands for Data Processing.

The encouraging factors

These are largely the opposite of the discouraging factors and include:

- Knowing 'why' – Why the work is done.
  Why the training is necessary.

- A friendly, helpful and understanding teacher.

- Clear examples and demonstrations.

- Encouragement – of the friendly kind.

Setting up on-job training

- Easy logical stages.

- Pleasant, comfortable surroundings.

- Plenty of humour to reduce tension.

Follow-up

Follow-up sessions with the trainee can be used to discuss the training and the trainee's subsequent progress. Such sessions will help by:

- Reinforcing the trainee's learning.

- Maintaining morale and enthusiasm.

- Providing an opportunity for identifying and solving problems.

Follow-up sessions should be informal and should be carried out about once a week for the first three months after training and less often, about once a month, after this. Each session should normally take 15–30 minutes.

The enterprising manager will find additional benefits in OJT. The preparation, consideration of job descriptions and so on, often reveal opportunities for improvements in job allocation and the like and can positively contribute to the success of the department.

A helpful source of information with how-to-do-it examples is the booklet *Management training by the Do-It-Yourself system*, published by The Industrial Society. Although this is concerned with the training of managers, the principles can equally well be applied to the training of non-managers.

14

GETTING OVER THE DELEGATION PROBLEM

Every manager agrees that delegation is a 'good thing' and we are all aware that the benefits of delegation can include:

- More time for the manager to plan ahead and deal with other strategically important matters.

- Improvement of job interest for those on the receiving end of delegation.

- Better distribution of work load.

- Less dependence on one or two people (who will retire one day).

- Faster development of up-and-coming individuals.

- Reduced Parkinsonism at lower levels (see page 114).

However, notwithstanding these enticing benefits, delegation tends to be neglected. If in doubt, ask the opinion of ambitious youngsters in any company or an O & M analyst – he will have found lack of proper delegation at the root of many of the problems he has been asked to solve.

The reasons for this neglect include (as stated by managers):

Getting over the delegation problem

- I have no time to delegate.

- I can do the work faster myself.

- I have delegated in the past and the result was a disaster.

- I don't know how to delegate.

The enterprising manager will take steps to avoid these situations.

Tackling the problem

The first essential stage for the enterprising manager is to make the psychological leap into deciding that delegation really *is* a good thing for all involved. The next step is to take on board a degree of self-discipline sufficient to decide that time *will* be made available. The result from this investment of time could be a massive dividend in time available to the manager himself at a later stage.

Having done this, the rest is technique.

Step 1

Examine your work load and identify the following:

- Work which consumes a significant amount of time but does not require any unusual expertise.

- Work which, if learned by others, would benefit all concerned in terms of faster departmental output, better absence cover or whatever.

- Work which does not fall readily into either of the above categories but which would improve the job interest and/or progress of a junior.

A list can then be made of these items of work; they are the jobs which potentially can be delegated.

Step 2

Consider the staff to whom work might be delegated and identify:

- Staff who would be likely to welcome more responsibility and could handle it.

- Those who would benefit from more experience and/or would find new experience motivating.

- Staff who are underemployed.

Some staff members may fit more than one of these categories but there may be others who are marginal cases for one or more of them. There could, for instance, be someone who might welcome more responsibility but there are doubts as to whether or not he could handle it. Unless the doubts are very strong and based on good reasons it pays to err on the side of giving such people the benefit. Most people are capable of rising to the occasion and the stimulating effect of more responsibility (or new experience) can bring out some surprising and unexpected abilities. Of course, this is not always the case but it is worth taking a chance on it as the reward for success can be high.

Step 3

Match the list from Step 1 with the names arising from Step 2 and prepare a programme for delegation. You will now have a list of work to be delegated and the names of people to whom the work will be allocated.

The delegation programme

This must include:

- A discussion with the employee to make sure he or she is willing to take on the new work. Some 'selling' may be necessary to overcome fears and lack of confidence but obviously this must not be overdone.

- A timetable for instruction – which *must* be completed *before* the work is handed over.

- A gentle handover arrangement, possibly in stages with opportunity for further instruction as any problems crop up.

The boss must not hand over the work without prior instruction and then leave the employee to struggle on. That is dumping, not delegation. Nor must he hand over the work properly but then interfere every five minutes. That destroys confidence. The keynote should be help and support with sympathetic understanding when mistakes are made.

The problems of the subordinate

The employee may face obstacles to accepting new work or persisting with it after the handover. The manager should be aware of them and allow for them. The obstacles are likely to be one or more of the following:

- It can be easier to ask the boss how to do a job than to sort it out oneself.

- Fear of criticism. (The subordinate may not do the work as skilfully as the boss.)

- Lack of information or skill, i.e. there has been a degree of dumping.

- Lack of confidence – usually overcome by good training.

- Lack of incentive – cash or otherwise.

A sympathetic response to any of these obstacles is required from the manager – who has a lot to gain from a successful delegation exercise.

A cautionary tale

Five departmental heads attended a meeting with a management consultant to discuss the possibilities of delegation. All five managers agreed that they were overworked and bogged down by trivia. However, whilst they all supported the idea of delegation *in principle*, four of them were convinced that their staff would not welcome delegated work. All five thought that their staff were already fully loaded and could not take on more work.

The consultant later talked with the staff in the department concerned. Twenty-seven out of 31 stated that they had time for more work and would welcome it. One stated that he was leaving the company to go to a more demanding job which would use his abilities more fully!

Parkinsonism

Parkinsonism is expressed in the aphorism 'Work expands so as to fill the time available for its completion'.

The author of this statement was the historian Cyril Northcote Parkinson who wrote the famous book *Parkinson's Law or the Pursuit of Progress* (John Murray, 1958). In his later book *The Law and the Profits* (John Murray, 1960), Parkinson described a second law which states that 'Expenditure rises to meet income'. This is also a law which provides thought for managers.

15

QUESTIONS OF DISCIPLINE

Discipline is more than a matter of time-keeping, demeanour in the workplace and ensuring that the company telephones are not used to make private calls to relatives in New Zealand. The manager must treat discipline as a wider subject. It includes sticking to the laid-down procedures and maintaining quality standards – and many other matters which will influence performance and profit.

Some managers encounter difficulty in maintaining discipline in personal behaviour and in the wider field of ways of working. The following are some guidelines for the manager experiencing such difficulties.

Commitment is essential

Very few normal, healthy and intelligent people will abide by rules which they do not understand and which seem to have no point. Even the most sensible rules can appear ridiculous (and there to be broken) if the purpose is not understood. This applies not only to particular individual rules but also to the whole network of do's and dont's which may be part of the working environment.

The first essential is to obtain the commitment of the staff to this network. This in turn requires their full understanding of the rules and the reasons why they are imposed.

IDEAS FOR ENTERPRISING MANAGERS

Commitment is best gained by drawing up the departmental requirements *jointly* between the manager and the staff. Some rules will of course be laid down by the company and the manager must explain the reason for them – however simple they may appear to be. The departmental rules such as the procedure for dealing with a document, how to deal with telephone enquiries and the like will probably lie within the scope of the manager's authority and these can be jointly agreed.

Once, by discussion, commitment of the staff has been obtained, the rules will be seen (a) less as rules to be broken and more as an agreement to be honoured and (b) as the framework of behaviour on which everyone depends.

In some situations the mutual dependency on everyone sticking to the rules is obvious – but should still be agreed. Not smoking on a filling station forecourt or in a paint store are examples. Less obvious are office procedures where, say, a clerk's failure to complete a form in full can result in someone else being inconvenienced or forced to carry out additional work. The need for disciplined working will be obvious to the person adversely affected but not necessarily to the offending clerk.

A brief discussion is all that is normally necessary to save oceans of problems for the manager, who might sum up the agreement with something along these lines:

> 'OK, George and Fred will always enter the product codes on the invoices before passing them to Sue so that she can look up the prices.'

In this expression the manager is stating the agreed rule, who is involved and the reason why.

A normally successful way to enforce such a rule if, after all, it is broken, is to swap the jobs around for a few days. If George or Fred spend some time doing some of Sue's work they will quickly learn why the procedure should be adhered to.

Questions of discipline

Avoid 'silly' rules

Patrick was head of a department of 12 people in an insurance company. Their work involved document processing but no contact with customers or other outsiders. Patrick was a somewhat old-fashioned character who disapproved of the younger generation in almost every aspect, but especially their styles of dress. No one would have blamed Patrick if he had forbidden his staff to wear punk outfits to the office but he actually insisted on plain white shirts and plain ties for the men and white blouses for the women. Rebellion ensued and Patrick spent much of his energy trying to enforce a rule which was not supportable and not endorsed by the company. Both morale and work suffered until Patrick's boss ordered him to drop the rules and to allow his staff to wear any reasonable dress that they wished.

Patrick also had a rule banning the use of calculators on the grounds that they made people lazy. Accuracy improved significantly when this rule was also abandoned. The fact is that silly rules will be treated with contempt – and deserve to be.

Keep the rules up to date

Circumstances change. What may have been a sensible rule long ago may now be pointless – or counterproductive. Check that every rule still has a valid reason. If there are one or two rules which do not have a valid reason they should be removed.

Avoid complicated rules

Every rule should be as brief and simple as possible and cover only one subject. A useful guideline is to avoid the kind of statements found in insurance policies, national legislation and local authority bye-laws. These are often so complicated and full of the words 'if', 'unless' and 'subject to' that they are either incomprehensible or capable of more than one interpretation.

Enforcing disciplined working

Hopefully, if the rules are easy to understand, the reason for them is clear. Many (if not all) will have been *jointly* worked out. The manager will have little trouble. A supportive, team atmosphere in the department can be so effective as to make any formal rules almost unnecessary. 'Almost' because there is the minority of people who will stray from the straight and narrow. It is for this minority that rules must be written and enforced.

The manager faced with a maverick employee must do all he can to deal with the problem himself and regard the use of any company disciplinary procedure as the last resort. Sometimes a re-statement of the reason for the rule will be enough to put things right; few people are so unreasonable or unintelligent as to be responsive only to threats or penalties. If they are, there is probably a fairly serious underlying problem such as domestic difficulties, financial worries or ill-health causing the person concerned to behave unreasonably – and probably untypically.

The explanation of the rule is likely to involve one of the following basic reasons for having the rule:

- Company image.

- Safety of the employees or outsiders.

- Efficiency and/or prevention of losses.

- The general welfare and mutual satisfaction of the employees as a whole.

Questions of discipline

In the event that a re-statement of the position has no effect the manager should look for any underlying problems before resorting to tougher measures. Such problems may be of a personal and private nature and the employee may not wish to reveal or discuss them. However, if the manager tactfully offers an opportunity for the problems to be discussed there is a good chance that it will be taken up.

Chloe, a competent secretary, was an example of someone whose work standards fell away due to private problems. She was taken to task by her boss for repeated errors in her work and, in particular, for arriving late in the morning. As her previous performance had been so good he eventually asked her if something was amiss. Chloe, with relief, explained that she was looking after her bed-ridden mother. This involved washing and feeding the mother each morning and then making arrangements for someone to look in on her during the day. This early morning activity often made Chloe late and caused her much worry. Once the situation had been explained and her boss expressed his sympathy and understanding, Chloe's work improved. Allowances were made for the early morning problems and the company organised help through the social services. The manager thus regained a dependable employee – one with even greater commitment to the job.

If all else fails, the various sanctions under the company disciplinary procedures may have to be involved. If so, this should be done without procrastination and as fairly and frankly as possible. It should be remembered that even an obvious undisciplined employee is likely to be viewed sympathetically by his or her colleagues if serious steps are taken. The manager must ensure that whatever happens is just and seen to be just and is carried out without delay. Delay provides time for rumours and attitudes to develop and allows people to lose sight of the original reasons why disciplinary action is justified.

16

THE MANAGER'S TIME

One of the most valuable resources available to the manager is his own time. It is important this is spent in the most productive way. But it is a great deal easier to say that time must be effectively used than it is to ensure that such is the case.

A group of four managers, each leading teams of around twelve people, all readily agreed during a training seminar that they were by no means certain that they were using their time effectively. Various problem areas were discussed such as time spent on paperwork, time spent reading, whether or not enough time was spent on planning and so on. None of them had any real idea how much time they were spending on the various aspects of their jobs or whether the split was in any way good or bad. It was decided that each of them would keep a diary record for ten days to take a sample of their work and see what amount of time was spent on each aspect.

The results were both surprising and worrying. The group *as a whole* found that their time was spent as follows:

Transactions	74%
Meetings	12%
Supervision and support of staff	4%
With clients	6%
Miscellaneous	4%

The manager's time

The two most dramatic figures were those for transactions, at 74 per cent, and supervision and support at 4 per cent. 'Transactions' was a term used to describe the work done for clients. Figures showed that the managers were so heavily involved in this activity as to leave inadequate time for the real management roles. With only 4 per cent of time being devoted to supporting their staff it was clear that there was a danger of both quality and quantity of work being allowed to deteriorate. Some of the time spent in meetings (12 per cent) could, at a stretch of the imagination, be termed planning but there was no apparent time allocated specifically to this function. In addition, the meetings were *all* outside the departments (e.g. with accountants to discuss budgets) which indicated a lack of communication with staff.

It was realised that the ten-day sample may have been unrepresentative but that the results were sufficiently significant to justify a check over a longer period. The four managers then repeated the exercise over five weeks – a period designed to encompass any variations which might be caused by a monthly cycle. At least two of the managers, for example, reckoned that each month end involved increased time spent on meetings.

The results of the longer trial revealed some differences in time allocation, including about 10 per cent on supervision and support of staff – compared with only 4 per cent in the first trial. However, it was agreed that this increase resulted from the shock caused by the 4 per cent result prompting the managers to spend more time with their staff. The main decision reached after consideration of the results was that the managers must spend much less time on transactions, delegate this work, and spend much more time with their staff teaching, guiding and monitoring. An arbitrary choice was made to spend at least 25 per cent of time with staff and no more than 40 per cent on transactions. Routine communication meetings were also agreed upon plus half a day each month in which the managers would review departmental progress and plan ahead.

With the exception of one manager who failed to extricate himself from his transactions, all found improvement in both work quantity and quality – and departmental morale. An interesting comment made by a number of staff was that the training and delegation had made their lives more interesting. They had previously nurtured a grievance that the managers kept all the really interesting transactions to themselves!

The case study indicates the potential value of keeping a record of how time is spent and then analysing the results in terms of the overall needs of the department. The manager can carry out his trial quite privately if he wishes and the result need not be a public embarrassment.

There can be no hard and fast rules about the amount of time to be spent on any particular activity as this will depend on the nature of the work and what must be accomplished. However, the manager can look for work which, in his judgement, is over-emphasised. Experience has shown that the following are fruitful areas for examination (in addition to those in the case study):

- Excessive paperwork – including pedantic records which serve no useful purpose, and defensive paperwork. The latter item includes the memoranda written to prove, in cases of trouble later, that something was done, someone was informed of something, etc.

- Time spent on fire-fighting. If this is a significant percentage it could indicate that the department is not sufficiently organised and/or that work is not carried out to a pre-agreed plan.

- Time spent on a recurring crisis, i.e. the same old problem crops up again and again. A clear indicator that a fundamental fault needs attention.

The manager's time

- Time spent sorting and summarising data by hand. This could be an ideal application for a computer system.

- Time spent detecting and correcting errors. Any substantial amount of time expended on this activity could mean that training is needed, systems and paperwork are faulty or simply that procedures are not being followed.

- Frequent occasions when *inconsequential* formal meetings and ad hoc discussions take place.

- A great deal of time on the telephone. The reasons should be examined to see if telephone technique is at fault. Or the telephone should be replaced by telex or some other non-voice means of communicating. If information can be sent or received by telex or fax it will not involve time spent in pleasantries or other non-essential talk.

If use of the telephone is essential it is helpful to:

(a) Have an alternative person in mind if your first choice is not available.

(b) Have a brief note made in advance on the subject of the conversation and all relevant papers and information on hand for reference.

(c) Avoid letting the ringing tone go on more than five or six rings.

(d) Avoid holding on if the person wanted is not immediately available.

Further reading

A useful book which delves further into the analysis of

IDEAS FOR ENTERPRISING MANAGERS

working practices and discusses priorities, planning for results and how to avoid procrastination is *Manage your Time, Manage your Work, Manage Yourself* by Donna Douglass (Kogan Page).

Part 3

The Paperwork Obstacle

Computers have not necessarily reduced paperwork. If it is not controlled it will clog the arteries of every organisation. The enterprising manager will not tolerate delays, errors and waste unnecessarily caused by faulty paperwork and the cumbersome systems that go with it.

The chapters in this part provide a complete kit for tackling the paperwork obstacle – the result of which can be a significant cost saving.

17

THE FIGHT AGAINST FORMS

'Whether forms increase or decrease the effectiveness of a procedure depends on the degree of care and skill with which they are designed. In the past their design has been all too often an afterthought.' These words were written in 1959 by G. E. Milward in his book *Organisation & Methods*. Experience in the subsequent years suggests that the problem is still with us. Paperwork has always been a happy hunting ground for the manager looking for ways to improve a department's operations.

In every organisation there are people inventing new forms. Some, possibly most, will be badly designed, unnecessary and time-wasting. They represent a potentially long-term drain on the efficiency of the people using them. All forms cost money – both to produce and to use – and it is well worth the manager's time to review them (say every 12 months) and root out unnecessary or unsatisfactory paperwork. The benefits can include:

- Reduction in expense.

- Reduction in labour.

- Enhanced efficiency.

- Reduction in errors (and the time required to correct them).

- Reduction in filing time and space usage.
- Reduction in frustration and irritation.

Asking the following questions, and acting upon the findings, will result in all or some of these benefits. Thorough investigation of forms commonly results in about a third of them disappearing for ever and another third being simplified or otherwise improved.

1. What is the purpose of the form? Is it necessary?

The form should have one or more of the following purposes:

- To store data.
- To communicate data.
- To process data (e.g. to calculate prices).

It will frequently be found that the original purpose has been lost or has become irrelevant over the years. In this case the form is a prime case for scrapping. However, assuming there is a clear purpose which has some value, then design of the form becomes important.

2. Are all the contents necessary?

Almost every form has a space (or spaces) for a date. This is often pointless. There may well be other items of data which are also painstakingly entered and which are not actually required and do not contribute to the agreed purpose of the form. In addition, there may be two or more forms with similar contents with consequent duplication of cost and effort.

The fight against forms

The X-chart is a simple tool to analyse the contents of forms and to indicate any waste. Duplication is readily revealed and the nature of the results can suggest streamlining or other improvements. Using the X-chart can indicate ways to get rid of forms and the clerical cost that goes with them.

The way to prepare an X-chart is shown in the following example:

Contents	Form A	Form B	Form C	Form D
Date	X	X	X	X
Invoice No.		X	X	
File No.	X			
Client's name	X	X	X	X
Client's address	X	X		
Discount				X
Price	X			X
Value				X
Description of goods	X	X		
Client's reference		X		
Stock code		X		

The X indicates that an item of data is given on the form or forms. By scrutiny the degree of overlap can be seen and a clue to methods of improvement is provided.

For example, the data of Form C appears on Forms A and B as well. Form C may therefore be unnecessary. Forms A and B have several common items and it may be possible to combine them. Having combined A and B, it might be possible to get rid of D – or combine it with A and B.

The X-chart may also show that a General Service Form can be introduced to replace a whole range of individual offerings. This will save both printing and stockholding costs.

3. Is the use of the form explained?

Errors often occur simply because instructions for the use of the form are not provided or are not clear. Ideally every form will be so simple as to be self-explanatory.

4. Is the form ambiguous?

One form in regular use asked for petrol consumption to be recorded in a box. Some people entered a number of gallons, others entered miles per gallon. The ambiguity could easily have been removed by pre-printing the abbreviation 'gals' on the form to show what was, in fact, required.

5. Are captions and column headings clear and appropriate?

A common fault is to make the column width accommodate the heading rather than the content. This results in a column headed *Code* being too narrow for a six-digit number and a column headed *Date of contract* being unnecessarily wide.

Large headings can sometimes be written diagonally, e.g.

[box with diagonal text: CONTRACT NO.]

or in layers, e.g.   CONTRACT
                        DATE

– in both cases to reduce the horizontal space used up.

6. Is the sequence of columns and spaces logical?

It is sometimes found, in forms used for calculation, that the space for the product of a multiplication precedes the multiplier and the multiplicand. The result of a calculation

The fight against forms

should, of course, be at the end of the sequence, e.g. $A \times B = C$ or $A - B = C$. Failure to place the various items in the sequence which people expect is a common cause of errors in calculation.

Similarly, like material is often best grouped together with like. This makes it easier to extract information from the form and might include say, personal details such as name, address, telephone number, date of birth and marital status.

7. Are multipart sets colour-coded?

This can help but they should also be numbered. The numbers are needed by the male staff of whom about 14 per cent will be to some extent colourblind – a point often overlooked by form designers.

It can also be helpful to mark each sheet with its purpose, e.g. File copy, Accounts copy, Customer copy. This improves the chances of correct distribution of the copies. It is also helpful when a system change takes place, in ensuring that any redundant copies are spotted or new requirements allowed for.

8. Is the paper right?

Heavy paper is usually more expensive than light paper and price also varies with quality. On the other hand, if the form is to be used outdoors, on the shop floor or in a warehouse, a heavier paper may well be necessary. A chemical factory once had a series of forms on flimsy paper. The forms literally tore to pieces in the wind when engineers tried to complete them standing on a gantry 100 feet above ground. Such considerations should be taken into account before printing the form and before the damage is done.

9. How will the form be filled in?

Typewriter? Word-processor? If so, the spaces and lines must it the typewriter. There is nothing more frustrating to the typist or more likely to cause errors than data spilling out of boxes or overflowing on to the line below.

Lines down should be ⅙ inch apart and character spaces should be:

> ¹⁄₁₀ inch for Pica machines.
> ¹⁄₁₂ inch for Elite machines.
> ¹⁄₁₆ inch for Petit Roman machines.

If the design is put together using a typewriter the correct spacing will be automatically achieved.

Handwriting? Lines should be ⅓ inch apart and character spaces ⅕ inch apart. Using this letter spacing means that typewriters can also be used if required.

Pencil? If so, a matt finish is helpful – as it is for ball-point pens. There is nothing more frustrating than trying to write on a glossy surface chosen because it makes the document appear more impressive.

10. Are boxes used for neatness, clarity and significance?

The use of boxes for answers enforces tidiness thus making the completed form more readable. Significant items such as grand totals, final costs etc. are easier to spot when placed in boxes having bold lines. Boxes (and columns) should be aligned to both stops if a typewriter is used.

11. Is fixed or recurring information pre-printed?

This saves clerical time and helps prevent errors of omission. Pre-printing also guarantees that an approved standard wording appears on every form rather than the variations likely if each user has a free choice.

12. Is data extracted for computer entry?

If so, as much as possible of the data to be picked up by the keyboard operator should be grouped together. Much time is lost and mistakes are caused when computer users have to dodge about from place to place on a form. In some cases it may be worth duplicating the appropriate entries by repeating them on a special key-punch section of the form. At all events the design of the form should be discussed with the people who must extract the data for computing purposes as well as the people who will fill in the form.

13. Is the form on standard-sized paper?

Your form may have been designed in the days of foolscap, quarto and double-elephant. If the change over to 'A' series paper has not been made it is likely that an unnecessarily high price is being paid for what is now a non-standard size.

Odd sizes, apart from cost, can cause other problems, e.g. the form may not fit window envelopes or file covers or filing cabinets.

In 1985 a company ordered special folders – at substantial cost – to take a form produced on non-standard paper (bought at a premium). The form was a relic of earlier days and, although its design was out of date, was being adhered to at all costs. Special filing cabinets were necessary in order to store the special folders resulting in expenditure almost double that required for standard-sized items.

14. Are there any unnecessary costly extras?

The following add extra cost:

- Perforation.

- Sequential numbering.

- Multi-colour printing.

- Embossing.

Discussion with the printer can be helpful in eliminating unnecessary and costly extras.

15. Are margins adequate?

Sufficient margin should be allowed for edge binding and clipping. Similarly, enough space should be left at top and bottom for the typist to fit the paper in her machine. Once again this is a case of carefully considering how the document will be used before finalising its design.

16. Are people's names printed on the form?

If so, remove them. A copy marked for *Chief Engineer* will not go out of date when Mr Blueprint (the Chief Engineer) retires or is promoted to Managing Director. A copy marked for Mr Blueprint will haunt him wherever he goes – leaving his successor without his copy!

Getting it right in the first place

Much trouble can be avoided by making sure that the form is properly designed before it comes into use and a lot can

The fight against forms

be achieved by taking into account the 16 points mentioned above, but the first essential step in designing a form is consultation:

Consult those responsible for the work giving rise to the form. Confirm purpose, validity of the purpose and every aspect of its intended use.
Consult those who will be associated with the form in any way, e.g. recipients in a branch office.
Consult, where practicable, those who will have to fill in the form.
Consult other users of similar forms, or forms designed to give the same or similar information. This may reveal that a suitable document already exists and/or will provide useful tips on design features.

With any luck, consultation will result in finding a way to do the job without introducing a new form at all and time, paper, money and storage space will be saved.

18

UNCLOGGING THE PAPERWORK DRAIN

The efficiency of clerical procedures normally involving a variety of forms, records and computer print-outs, can determine the effectiveness of the company. A badly organised system can delay production, delay deliveries, annoy customers and cost money. A good system, on the other hand, can result in a vital edge over the competition and substantially increased profit.

The enterprising manager, keen to ensure that his procedures are efficient, will find that it is not difficult to analyse what is happening with the flow of paper in his department – and that the results can be dramatic.

A real-life case

Sinkem and Drownem Shipping Company had a problem in that too much time elapsed before the required debit notes and other documents emerged from the clerical process. Repeated increases in staff in the various departments (the usual reflex action to a problem of delay) had yielded no improvement. Not only were S and D losing income from late debiting but customer service was suffering too.

It was decided to have a detailed look at what happened from the time the first activity took place to the time the final documents were produced. One experienced man-

Unclogging the paperwork drain

ager was given the job of analysing the system and he used the 'organisation and methods' technique of asking:

- What is done?

- Who does it?

- Where is it done?

- When is it done?

- How is it done?

In addition to each of these questions, the further question 'why' was posed.

Each person and department visited was asked these questions in turn and the various documents traced from person to person and place to place. The results were recorded and a chart drawn up showing how the documents moved and what work was done on them at each of the various stages. The resulting chart looked like this:

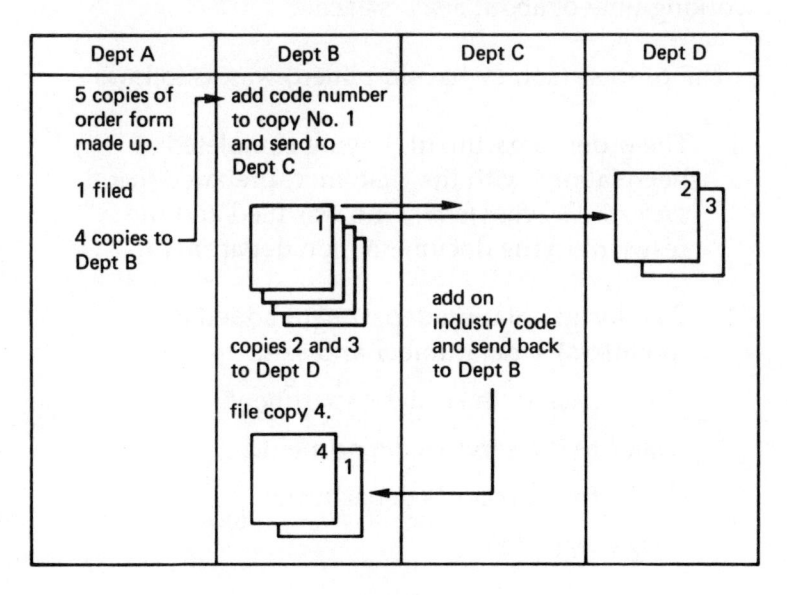

Dept A	Dept B	Dept C	Dept D
5 copies of order form made up. 1 filed 4 copies to Dept B	add code number to copy No. 1 and send to Dept C copies 2 and 3 to Dept D file copy 4.	add on industry code and send back to Dept B	

IDEAS FOR ENTERPRISING MANAGERS

The chart, using pictures of the forms, showed, at a glance, who did what and where. The arrows showed the various movements. The following discoveries were made:

- Nine departments and a senior manager were involved in the process.

- The senior manager received dozens of documents each week but did nothing with them – a fact which astonished the heads of the departments when they were informed of it.

- The original documents moved 14 times and joined 11 queues.

Note: Every time a document leaves one person or place and goes to another person or place it joins a queue. That is to say it will wait for some period of time before being dealt with. The sum of the waiting time normally far exceeds the working time. It was for this reason that a London broking house was finding *elapsed* times of up to *120 days* in completing documents which required a working time of about *6 hours* each.

The process (somewhat simplified) was as follows:

1. The order department, having completed negotiations with the customer, prepared *five copies of the order form*. One was filed and the rest sent to the documentation department.

2. The documentation department added a (pointless) serial number and sent:

Copy 2 back to the order department

Copy 1 to the services department

Copy 3 to the records department

Copy 4 was filed.

Unclogging the paperwork drain

> **Summary:** (a) The order department now had two copies on file, one of which had a meaningless serial number. (b) The documentation department had a file copy (never to be used again).

3. Services department filed their copy (*Copy 1*).

4. Records department added various code numbers to their copy (*Copy 3*) and sent it to the senior manager.

5. The senior manager kept *Copy 3* for some time then, having done nothing with it, sent it back to the records department.

    > **Comment:** Rumour had it that many years ago the senior manager's predecessor checked the copies. The present incumbent did no checking but held on to each *Copy 3* until he had a bundle of them. He then sent them back.

    > **Summary:** (c) The services department now have a file copy (useless). (d) Some days have been lost whilst copies were in the senior manager's queue.

6. Records department added more numbers to *Copy 3* (now in batches) and sent them to accounts department.

7. Accounts department added a *debit note code* and sent the batches to services department.

8. Services department added *payment instructions* and sent the batches to finance department.

    > **Summary:** (e) More time lost in queues. (f) Services department have added payment

[139]

instructions which they could have added at an earlier stage when they received *Copy 1* (which so far has served no purpose).

9. Finance department add certain cash values and send the batches (still *Copy 3*) to the statistics department.

10. Statistics department extract data and send the batches to records department (who had the documents at stage 6).

    Summary: (g) yet more queues.

11. Records department now prepare two key punch documents for the computer department, *photocopy* the forms before sending the photocopies to the order department and then file the forms (never to be seen again).

    Summary: (h) More queuing. (i) Order department now have 2 copies on file plus a photocopy showing code numbers etc. added in the meantime.

12. The computer department key-punch the data received and produce the required output documents including the debit note.

    Summary: (j) At last the required result is achieved after yet another queue in the computer department.

The result

Scrutiny of this muddle (almost impossible without the chart) showed that:

- The order form itself could with slight amendment be used as a key-punching document, thus cutting out the creation of two forms in stage 11.

- The order form sets could be sent from the order department direct to the records department (cutting out two queues) and thence to the finance department, who also add the debit note code formerly added by accounts. This saved more queues including the delay in the senior manager's office.

- A copy could be sent to the statistics department at the *end* of the process when all other work was done thus cutting out yet another queue.

The net result of the study was to reduce the elapsed time from about three months to an average of 10 days. Further refinement at a later stage reduced the time to an average of three working days. Eventually, after the re-training of certain staff who hitherto had no real understanding of what the work was all about, a standard time of two working days was successfully achieved.

The lessons to be learned

- Too many bits of paper can be sent to and from too many departments. Every time one of these movements is cut out valuable time is saved.

- Tidying up the system can reduce the number of copies made and filed – including photocopies.

- Concentrating as many small functions as possible into one place saves time and can also result in fewer errors being made.

- No one should receive documents if they do nothing with them – or nothing worthwhile.

IDEAS FOR ENTERPRISING MANAGERS

The example described is by no means untypical. Any lengthy clerical process when closely examined is likely to yield some beneficial results. Not untypical either was the surprise expressed by the people in the departments involved when the whole picture was revealed to them. Individual departments had no way of seeing the total picture and could only control their own parochial activities. Had the man in overall charge been an enterprising manager he could have sorted out the mess – or at least stopped forms coming to him when he had no intention of doing anything with them.

19

REDUCING CLERICAL ERRORS

Clerical errors still occur, despite the fact that in modern times most problems are blamed on computer error. In fact, all computer errors are human errors caused by programmers, data-entry staff and, among others, clerks. Computers are as incapable of making mistakes as typewriters are of making a spelling mistake. It is to the activities of the human being that we must look for the causes of mistakes.

It is not old-fashioned therefore for the enterprising manager to seek ways and means of reducing clerical errors. The key lies in knowing what the causes are and preventing the errors by dealing with these causes. The check-list of possible causes which follows is based on real-life experience in a variety of situations and, hopefully, will give the manager a programme of action which will at least halve the problem.

1. *Poor supervision*

Good supervision reduces mistakes. Too many clerical supervisors are given the job without any prior training. Frequently the oldest, longest serving clerk is promoted to supervisor when the previous incumbent retires or drops dead. Long-serving clerks, especially when they have no supervision training, are not always the best people to lead others. The first step in such cases is to provide the necessary training.

External courses are recommended (e.g. those provided by The Industrial Society) to ensure that the supervisor has a working knowledge of at least the following:

- Control of work loads and monitoring throughput.

- Motivating staff.

- On-job training methods.

- Induction of new employees.

- Forms design.

- The intelligent use of office machinery.

In addition, the supervisor must have a sound technical knowledge of the work of the department *and* of other associated departments with whom they may be interdependent.

Having, hopefully, satisfactorily increased the capabilities of the existing supervisors, the manager should consider preventative measures for the future. Any future promotional appointment should result from a planned programme of recruitment, training and appraisal such that junior staff with supervisory ability are identified and prepared in advance. Merely promoting the next person in line or the oldest inhabitant may well be the worst possible choice.

2. Unsuitable staff

One of the senior managers of a major British company insisted that all of his clerical staff be of 'A'-level standard of education. He was puzzled by the high turnover of clerks in his various departments and the poor quality of their work until it was pointed out to him that 'A'-level people were bored by the (to them) undemanding nature of the work. In addition, many were ambitious and could see nothing ahead but years of tedious routine and, in consequence, were not motivated to do a good job of work.

In other words, he recruited at too high a level. The opposite can also apply. The manager should set standards for recruitment suitable to the work to be done.

A basic knowledge of mathematics and English is the bedrock requirement. Existing staff without such knowledge might well be motivated by in-house training to reach the right level. Staff who are stimulated and working at the right level for their abilities and ambitions make fewer errors.

3. Poor systems

Badly designed forms (see Chapter 17), insufficient equipment, out-of-date or cumbersome procedures, and unnecessary accuracy demands all help to increase mistakes. A thorough look at paperwork and procedures is recommended (see Chapter 18).

4. Uneven distribution of work

Most large offices have a 'willing horse' among the staff; the cheerful easy-going character in the corner who is always willing to take on another chore. The supervisor, being human, will be tempted to pass that irksome extra job to the willing horse time after time. The effect of this is twofold: a lazy attitude on the part of the other clerks who will emulate the supervisor whenever they can, and overwork for the willing horse.

Errors increase with fatigue and pressure and uneven distribution of work can result in these effects. Continued abuse of the willingness of the individual ultimately results in a sense of grievance. This attitude spreads and poor work multiplies. Supervisors must allocate work on an equitable basis, in particular doing everything possible to avoid prolonged pressure on any individual.

This is the type of problem which a supervisor can learn to avoid by attending a training course. But experience shows that it is a problem which someone else, looking at the department from the outside, is more likely to spot. The enterprising manager should be in a good position to do it.

5. Bad working conditions

There are still a few Dickensian sweat-shops to be found – badly lit, cold, draughty and often dirty. There are also supposedly modern offices which, whilst clean and flashy, have ventilation and humidity problems which reduce work quality.

In one such office in a European capital almost all the staff felt drowsy after a couple of hours or so at their desks. Trips to the coffee machine were made with remarkable frequency throughout the day. Most of the staff did not want the coffee but needed to move around to keep alert!

The problem was solved when the office was redesigned to improve ventilation and to break up the monotonous rows of glass-walled boxes which people sat in. The effect of this layout had been hypnotic. The fact is that errors decrease when such discomforts and distractions are removed and staff are provided with decent conditions.

Having ensured the highest possible degree of comfort the manager might also consider the question of personal breaks. Coffee breaks – especially if taken away from the desk or machine – reduce fatigue and boredom. The timing of the break is also important. Not everyone needs refreshment at the same time and if possible the usual beverages should be available at all times. Vending machines are useful in providing freedom of choice both in terms of time and beverage. Fears that staff will spend all day at the drinks vendor have been disproved by users who in fact enjoy the high output of more lively staff.

6. Vague instructions (or none at all)

The clerk who is left to muddle through as best he or she can is almost certain to make mistakes.

Every office from time to time receives the once-off job or special exercise. Some supervisors will fail to obtain clear instructions from their superiors and, worse still, hand the job to one of the clerks with only a vague indication of what is required.

Similarly, routine tasks tend to pass from one person to another as the requirements of holiday and sickness absences dictate. The recipient of handed-over work is particularly vulnerable to errors in the early stages. Clearly written procedure manuals should be available for regular office jobs and, in every case, supervisors must ensure by personal discussion that the clerk fully understands what is required.

The enterprising manager will check to see that all routine procedures are written up (up to date) with sample forms and other visual aids and that this information is readily available to all.

20

OFFICE MECHANISATION – POINTS TO WATCH

From time to time one comes across cases where office mechanisation has been introduced on the basis that 'it must be a good idea'. This can be a costly error. It is important to study the situation carefully, including the work concerned, weighing up the pros and cons before opting for mechanisation. There are some types of work, for example, where the alternative courses of action are so varied that only very expensive mechanisation (such as a large computer) would adequately cope with the situation. Conversely, some work is so simple and requires so little time that using a machine to do it is like using the proverbial sledge-hammer to crack a nut.

Generally speaking, mechanisation pays off where work is repetitive, easily defined and high in volume. Manual (human) application is generally more desirable where work varies, requires judgement and the procedures are liable to frequent short-notice change. A typical mechanisation situation, for example, is a simple payroll involving pay slips, records and preparation of pay cheques. All these requirements can be produced rapidly and simultaneously by a machine with little chance of error. A human (non-mechanical) process might be preparation of legal documents where the wording is appropriate to each case individually.

Office mechanisation – points to watch

Possible benefits of mechanisation

- *Cost saving*. Mechanisation can reduce labour costs, providing that enough repetitive work is involved and the procedures are properly planned.

- *Improved accuracy*. Accuracy in calculations can be gained. An example can be found in automatic production of invoices where price extensions can be machine-calculated inclusive of discount and/or commission calculations. Such calculations are error prone when carried out by human beings.

    Similarly, accuracy in copying can be achieved by using photographic or mechanical devices. For example, a cheque can be automatically written as part of a process involving payroll or payables ledgers. Use of the mechanical system will ensure that the amount shown on the cheque will be the same as the amount shown on the payroll ledger.

    Other ways to achieve error reduction which mechanisation can offer are the use of hash totals, check digits and other arithmetic devices for detecting an error (such as an impossible code number) before any damage is done. Precautions of this sort can be programmed into the system so that the machine will faithfully apply them to each transaction.

- *Reduced drudgery*. A well-chosen mechanical system can relieve the human being of boring repetitive work, leaving him or her free for work requiring the human brain. This improves job interest and morale.

- *Speed*. Machines are generally faster in operation than human beings and they do not slow down due to fatigue or need to take a break.

- *Spin-offs*. It is sometimes possible to mechanise a job and then find an additional advantage. A sales ledger posting system may, after mechanisation, be capable of producing sales analyses without additional work. The machine, when posting to the ledger, can record the items simultaneously on a paper or magnetic record, building up the analyses as the work goes along. Such spin-off benefits should be looked for when considering or planning a mechanised system – sometimes the extra benefit will make all the difference to the economics of the system.

Possible disadvantages of mechanisation

- High set-up costs. A capital outlay may be required – although most items of office machinery can be hired or leased. Tax considerations will need to be looked into.

- Work input for the machine must be in a suitable form. This may mean additional labour costs on preparation of the input data. Similarly, the data put into the system must be correct. If errors can be automatically detected the damage is prevented but correction still takes time. If the errors cannot be corrected they will be processed – at high speed.
  The old adage 'Garbage in, garbage out' holds good.

- More discipline in associated clerical operations is required. This is often a substantial *benefit* but can be difficult to achieve. Forms, for example, must be fully and correctly completed. The machine, unlike the human being, cannot exercise imagination or initiative and make allowance for an omission.

- The machine may not be sufficiently utilised. There is little point in buying a machine if it is not economically used.

- Operator training may be difficult and cover may be needed for holiday, sickness and other absences.

- Special forms or other stationery may be needed. These supplies, being specially manufactured, are likely to be more expensive than run-of-the-mill supplies.

Office mechanisation – points to watch

The enterprising manager's checklist

Taking into account all the factors already pointed out in this chapter, the manager contemplating mechanisation of an office procedure should work through the following checklist to help him decide whether to go or not to go:

- Is there a positive benefit to be gained which outweighs any disadvantage (e.g. speed, accuracy or cost saving)?

- Is the machine fast enough for the volumes? Remember the peaks and troughs in volumes of work reaching the machine. Manufacturers quoted speeds may not be achievable in practice and may not be enough to cope with peak periods.

- Can operators (including standby operators) be readily trained?

- How much help will the manufacturer or supplier give (e.g. with installation and training)?

- Is there a fast, reliable maintenance service? The supplier's repair service must be fast enough to prevent a crisis when a breakdown occurs.

- Are there environmental problems – noise, heat? Will air-conditioning, cooling or sound-proofing be needed?

- What additional costs will arise (e.g. special stationery, magnetic disks)?

- How soon will the system be obsolescent, e.g. will the machine pay for itself before spare parts and maintenance become unavailable?

A satisfactory answer to all the questions in the checklist will be a clear go-ahead signal. In most cases in real life there will be one or more unsatisfactory answers and the manager will need to exercise some common-sense judgement.

21

FINDING TIME TO READ

The majority of managers receive trade journals, technical reports, financial newspapers, etc., to read. Finding the time to read them can be a problem. As often as not, the job is neglected or left until the information is out of date. This happens despite the fact that it is important for many managers to keep up to date with the activities of customers and competitors, foreign exchange rates, share prices and, in the case of managers involved in exporting, overseas political and business news. Failure to spot some significant items of news can result in missed opportunities or problems for the business. A simple solution to the problem – which also helps to speed up the circulation of the reading matter – is the 'A and B-reader' system.

How the system works

For each journal an 'A-reader' is appointed. This reader is a *junior* who is briefed on the topics that the 'B-readers' are interested in and who works methodically through every page of the journals, newspapers, etc., ignoring the junk but identifying the useful articles. The pages which should be read by the B-readers are then marked by the A-reader on a circulation slip and the journal passed to them.

This process enables the B-readers to go straight to the

items of interest to them without wasting time on irrelevant or otherwise useless material.

An additional benefit to be gained from this system is that the A-reader receives a form of training. Regular reading of the appropriate business literature over a period of months can significantly add to the knowledge and understanding of younger employees.

A fast-circulation variation

Some companies have found an additional advantage in arranging for the A-reader to photocopy articles and send the photocopies to the appropriate B-reader rather than the whole publication. This results in the information reaching the B-readers earlier than if they had to wait their turn on a circulation slip. This increases the chances of the manager having enough time to act effectively as a result of the knowledge he has gained and reduces the frustration of finding things out too late.

A-readers should be encouraged to read the advertisements as well as the articles as this can yield useful information on what competitors and customers are doing. The appearance of an advertisement for a new service or product is sometimes the first inkling of a competitor's actions. The earlier it is known about, the earlier a response can be made.

Another potentially fruitful source of knowledge, often neglected, are the job advertisements. A company in the insurance industry was first warned of a competitor entering the market by an advertisement for a specialist in a particular type of insurance. The A-reader who spotted the advertisement was estimated to have given his company 3–6 months' prior warning of the competitor's intentions.

22

CUTTING DOWN ON REPORTS

When Grandfather ran the company, he decided what information was needed. Executive decisions descended from his office based on one set of reports which he demanded and only he received. The growth of the company and the departure of Grandfather have given rise to the delegation of his responsibilities to a variety of people, all of whom have their own idea of the information needed to execute their duties.

The result is frequently a complex network of reports, summaries and tabulations prepared in varying ways and reporting much the same information to different people in many different places. Some of the information may be unnecessary, some of doubtful accuracy and, probably, much of it is received too late to be of anything but academic interest – which is possibly misleading.

Apart from the damage that can arise from misleading reports, an ever-increasing cost is incurred in producing them.

What can be done about it?

Every company must have a carefully designed system of integrated control of its activities to ensure that resources are most profitably applied. To plan and implement such a

Cutting down on reports

system may need many months and possibly two or three years of intensive work. The enterprising manager will be looking for a faster result. Fortunately, much can be done by a team of two or perhaps three people in a period of three to six months, depending on the size and organisation of the company.

The essential objective of the team should be to uncover and itemise all the information produced and recorded for management within the company. Surprising results may be expected, although perhaps less dramatic than one company where an O & M analyst discovered that the staff provided the managing director with no fewer than 800 reports each month. Naturally few of these were actually read or acted upon.

It is absolutely vital that the study be initiated at board level. The top stratum of executives is normally at the apex of the reporting pyramid and it is at this apex that policy decision-making is concentrated. Additionally, staff at all levels must be fully aware that the investigation has board level approval and will receive board level consideration.

If possible, only two staff members should form the study team, although three may be necessary if much time is likely to be consumed in travelling. The smaller the team the more likely it is that the information gathered will be fully understood – and the cost of the study will be less.

There are no hard and fast rules as to the type of investigator required but the following attributes are desirable:

- A good general knowledge of the company.
- A widely acceptable 'desk-side manner'.
- Previous organisation-and-methods experience.
- Some knowledge of accounting.
- Imagination, curiosity and a measure of cynicism.

- Ability to absorb detail without losing sight of the broad picture.

- Middle management status or an equivalent 'presence'.

Clear terms of reference should be provided to the team, in writing. Without exception all staff should be aware in advance that the study is to be made. Full details should be given to them of the intentions and the timing with as much information as possible on the way the study will be conducted and, most important, why.

Inadequate publicity wastes time and tends to give rise to damaging rumours about redundancy or other fears. Also, many supervisors, section leaders and managers really do need advance warning to find out what goes on in their departments. There are heads of departments who sincerely believe the most astonishing fictions about the activities of their own staff. Announcements should preferably be identifiable as having come from the chairman or managing director and at all events be clearly board level statements.

Planning

The team will need time to prepare its programme in order to avoid duplication or gaps and to work out a uniform method of obtaining information. The following points are suggested for inclusion in the planning stage:

- If no organisation chart is available – or the existing one is out of date – a diagram of company structure should be prepared. Areas of responsibility should be at least broadly defined.

- Based on the organisation chart, the interviewing work can be divided among team members in such a way that the investigations will follow a logical pattern. For

Cutting down on reports

example, staff responsible directly or indirectly to the marketing director should all be interviewed by the same member of the team, and not by whoever is available at the time.

- A standard set of questions should be drawn up to form a basis for questioning. Possible topics include: the nature of the problems the subject deals with and the decisions he is required to make; the information that is ideally needed to deal with the subject's decisions and problems; and the information that the subject *actually* gets and his opinion of that information.

  Time spent in analysing the interviews will be reduced if a standard form for answers is designed.

Each senior executive should be visited and questioned before any of his subordinates are interviewed. Every scrap of information that contributes to providing a picture of the subject's job must be recorded.

Most important of all is to find out what happens to the reports the subject receives. Does the information really provoke action or is it 'just for information'? Does the subject give the reports detailed study? Does he (or his secretary) take extracts for recording elsewhere? If extracts are taken, what is done with them?

The nature and content of *each* report require study in detail. Copies should be obtained and examined for degree of accuracy, age of the data, style of presentation and all other aspects which may have a bearing on the cost and the value of the report to the company. Much cross-checking may be required since it is not a rarity for an executive to be on the receiving end of a report without being aware of it. Secretaries sometimes file away routine reports without the executive always being aware of their existence. The investigator must therefore not only record the reports received but also the reports issued.

Interviewers should gradually work down the scale to the source of each document. Careful records should be made of the files, ledgers, record cards, little black books and other documents maintained in order to provide management information.

Wherever possible, an estimate should be made of the cost of the various records kept. This can most conveniently be expressed in terms of the man-hours of work needed to create and maintain them, with any obvious additional charges such as computer time and stationery costs.

Analysis

The records, when collected, can be divided into a suitable set of categories, and then a comparison should be made to determine the degree of duplication.

The same data may be prepared in two places (or twice by the same person) in varying degrees of accuracy. This can arise where the original report was required with, say, cash figures rounded off, but was subsequently demanded by one executive without rounded figures. Such cases are quite common and result in an increased cost of preparation. It is precisely this type of extra cost that needs to be challenged.

Having listed the duplication, charts should be prepared illustrating the flow of information. Separate charts may be used to illustrate the origin and ultimate destinations of groups of records and reports all relating to the same category of data. Opportunities may be revealed where separate reports can be merged.

The charts should be backed up with written notes drawing attention to the areas where savings can be made and also to any anomalies in the content of reports.

Data that cannot or do not give rise to action should be highlighted. This would include reports that remain with the originator or are quietly filed away after preparation. Cases where the data passes through such a long processing chain as to be out of date when completed should also be listed and the reasons for delay clearly described.

Cutting down on reports

The investigating team will find it helpful to list separately all reports which it believes require reconsideration. Generally these reports will fall into the following groups:

- Duplications (or triplications).

- Out of date when completed.

- Do not result in any form of action.

- Produced in an unnecessarily costly manner.

- Containing irrelevant matter.

- Confusing and difficult to understand.

- Unnecessary copies for information.

Further categories may be discovered, all of which should be reported along with an estimate of their cost in terms of man-hours to prepare. The investigators should not forget to include in the cost figure all the work down the chain that leads to the final preparation of each report.

Having completed the analysis, the team will prepare a report to management stating its findings. As far as possible this report should be illustrated with charts and examples and backed up by suggestions on how to bring about improvements whenever these are possible.

Using the results

There are all too many temptations to avoid action. Fears of upsetting the more conservative managers, complacency and sheer inertia can all produce inaction. To ensure action is taken, one or at most two top executives should be given authority to implement changes.

Management should *not* do the following:

- State that 'we must not act too rapidly'. This avoids the necessity of getting started.

- Set up an alternative for every proposal. This results in no action or the wrong action.

- Wait to consult an expert.

- Issue a statement announcing that 'management problems have been clarified, new vistas opened, our inventiveness challenged, but a further study is required of other related problems before any decisions can be made'.

What can the enterprising manager do by himself?

The point has been made that a study such as described in this chapter is ideally of a company-wide nature and supported at board level. The departmental or divisional manager who cannot interest his colleagues in a company-wide study can scale down the operation and carry it out within his own area of responsibility. Care must be taken when doing this to ensure that information flowing out of the department or division is not arbitrarily cut off as this could be disastrous to another part of the company. However, some checking with colleagues might well reveal that they would not object to some cost-saving changes (e.g. some of the data sent to them may, on examination, turn out to be a waste of effort). At least the manager can ensure that nothing he gets is in any way unnecessary or undesirable.

Part 4

Help from Simple Maths

Job advertisements for managers often demand 'a high degree of numeracy'.

While quite a few of us are not really sure what is meant by numeracy, it is certain that some simple arithmetical techniques are a valuable part of the enterprising manager's repertoire.

The arithmetic in Part 4 is not complicated and the enterprising manager without a PhD in higher mathematics will find it useful and useable.

23

BREAK-EVEN POINT – AND ITS USES

Small, young businesses are particularly prone to failure due to an inability to get prices right and to see the relationship between fixed costs, variable costs and income.

Fixed costs are those which the business is stuck with regardless of how much production is completed or sales made, and include such items as:

- Rent of premises.
- Insurances.
- Equipment leasing costs.

Since employees cannot be hired and fired at will, wages and salaries should be regarded as a fixed cost – at least in the short term.

Variable costs are those which are incurred only when production is carried out (or a service provided) and are roughly proportional to the volume of product or service. Variable costs can include:

- Raw materials.
- Electricity.
- Delivery charges.

IDEAS FOR ENTERPRISING MANAGERS

Both types of costs must be covered by earnings and every business needs to know what it must do to achieve this. As an example, let us consider a one-man mini-cab business in a quiet rural area.

The fixed costs of the business will include say:

Depreciation of the car	£1,000 p.a.
Tax	£ 100 p.a.
Insurance	£ 500 p.a.
Other	£ 50 p.a.
	£1,650 p.a.

The owner of the business must therefore earn £1,650 to cover his fixed costs. However, earning this amount is not enough. He must also earn enough to cover the variable costs which will occur whenever he takes the car on the road. These costs will include say:

Petrol	10p per mile
Oil	1p per mile
Tyres etc.	1p per mile
Maintenance	2p per mile
	14p per mile

So for every mile he drives the driver must earn 14p to cover his variable costs *plus* enough to cover his fixed costs.

The fixed costs must be allocated over all the miles he does. One of his major problems will be to decide how many miles he must do. In other words, how much business he must do to break even – and subsequently make a profit. In addition, he will have competitors who will be charging a certain price. Obviously he cannot easily exceed this price unless he has some additional (and saleable) service to offer.

By calculating the break-even point, based on the regular

Break-even point and its uses

market prices, the owner of the business can see what he must do to make a profit, and how much profit he will make at various levels of activity. A simple table of figures is all that is needed.

Assuming that the price which can be charged per mile is 25p then the costs and earnings of our car-hire business will work out as follows:

Miles done	Fixed costs £	Variable costs £	Total costs	Income	Profit/ Loss
1,000	1,650	140	1,790	250	1,540 L
5,000	1,650	700	2,350	1,250	1,100 L
10,000	1,650	1,400	3,050	2,500	550 L
15,000	1,650	2,100	3,750	3,370	380 L
20,000	1,650	2,800	4,450	5,000	550 P
25,000	1,650	3,500	5,150	6,250	1,100 P
30,000	1,650	4,200	5,850	7,500	1,650 P

Examination of the table will tell the proprietor of the business that if he charges a standard 25p per mile he will make a loss if he does less than about 16,000 miles in a year. He can also see how many miles he must do to make varying levels of profit. He can work out how many miles he must do to produce a profit which is worth his while. He can then also calculate if this worthwhile level of profit is achievable at all!

Suppose that he anticipates 10 journeys per day of 5 miles on average (e.g. picking up customers from the station), and 1 journey per day of 30 miles (a trip to the airport). The rest of his time will be spent waiting for customers (during which time he washes his car).

His earnings will be:

```
        10 journeys at 10 miles = 100 miles
         1 journey at 30 miles  =  30 miles
                                  ─────
                                  130 miles per day
                                  ═════
```

IDEAS FOR ENTERPRISING MANAGERS

He can see from the table that he must do about 16,000 miles in a year to reach his break-even point so his first conclusion is that he reaches this point after working for

$$\frac{16,000}{130} = 123 \text{ days}$$

He can also see that at 130 miles per day he will earn 130 × 25p = £32.50 per day.

If he reckons that allowing for bad weather, competition, public holidays, sickness and days when the car is being serviced he will work for 4 days a week, then he will work for 4 × 52 = 208 days a year. From this he will earn 208 × £32,50 = £6,750. From the table he will see that the profit left over after costs of about £5,500 will be about £1,250.

He might draw the following conclusions:

- £1,250 is not enough to live on and he would be better off finding something else to do. Even if he can do 50 per cent more work, or can increase his price to, say, 30p per mile, he will not make a fat living.

- If he invested the amount he must spend to buy the car (say £7,000) in a building society, we would make around £560 per year, without doing any work at all!

- If he could operate his business in a busy urban area he might do much better.

- He might achieve a more attractive level of profit if he can reduce his fixed costs, e.g. by buying a smaller car or by doing his own maintenance.

He must examine the feasibility of these alternatives.

The above example indicates some of the uses of the break-even point, viz.:

Break-even point and its uses

- Determining the volume of business necessary to achieve a profit.

- Estimating the profit (or loss) which is likely to be made at various levels of production.

Information of this sort will enable the manager to:

- Decide if a project under consideration is likely to be worthwhile.

- See if the project is soundly based or whether fixed costs are too high, the business is in the wrong area, the price necessary to make a worthwhile profit is too high for customers to accept, etc.

Additions to resources – should it be done?

Re-calculation of the break-even point can be valuable in cases where a business is considering expanding its resources by renting larger premises, buying more machinery or taking on more employees. Any of these will cause a jump in fixed costs which will make it necessary to increase output to stay at the same profit level. In other words, the break-even point is pushed further away.

It is entirely possible to make a profitable business unprofitable by additions to fixed costs – a situation which might well be avoided if the break-even point is re-calculated and the implications carefully considered. There is not much point in, say, renting more space, if the increase in costs necessitates production and sales rising by 50 per cent in a market which offers too few customers to meet the level of output.

Alternatively it might be seen that the level of business necessary to cover the cost of the new premises can only be achieved with more machinery and labour – adding yet more fixed costs and pushing the break-even point even further away.

A thought on reducing selling price

Obviously the selling price must cover both fixed and variable costs with something left over for profit. There are, however, occasions when a price below this level is justified.

Take, for example, the manager of a hotel who finds at 8.00 p.m. that he has a third of his bedrooms empty. Let us assume that his room-rate is £20 per night and at this price he makes a profit of £5. His variable costs per room, covering soap, laundry and other oddments (i.e. the costs incurred only if a guest uses a room) are, say, £2.

If a late arriving traveller wants a room but will only pay £10 what should the hotel manager do? The answer is that he should accept the £10 offer because although *he will not make a profit* he will cover his variable costs and have a further £8 as a contribution to his unavoidable fixed costs.

The rule for the manager is to accept a price above variable costs providing:

- The resources causing the fixed costs would otherwise be under-used.

- Longer-term considerations, such as setting a new, unprofitable, market price are taken into account.

- No one imagines that a true profit is being made. This has been the downfall of many businesses.

The enterprising manager can apply the break-even concept to a variety of situations, such as considering the purchase of office or factory machinery, and can also use the break-even calculation to justify a request for capital

Break-even point and its uses

expenditure. Likewise by working out the figures the manager who is considering approaching his company for more money in his budget may find that either:

- His demands cannot be justified, in which case he can avoid an embarrassing encounter with the company accountants.

or
- He needs to take some other action (perhaps reorganising the production process) before he can reach a position where his request will stand up to scrutiny.

24

PINPOINTING THE PROBLEM (OR OPPORTUNITY)

Lloyd's (the insurance market, not the bank) made a record underwriting loss in 1982. In his comments on the figures, the Chairman of Lloyd's said: 'Virtually all our losses came from an area that provides 12 per cent of the premium.'

This real-life example illustrates the principle behind the *80–20 Rule* – a simple concept which provides the enterprising manager with an easy technique for spotting the cause of a problem or an opportunity to be exploited. The 80–20 Rule, also known as *Pareto's Principle*, is a recognition of the fact that a small number of factors in a situation often account for a large proportion of the effect. For example, 80 per cent of sales may be achieved by only 20 per cent of the salesmen. Alternatively, 75 per cent of sales servicing costs may be caused by only 10 per cent of the customers. This latter example might suggest that much more profit could be achieved by dropping all or some of the 'bad 10 per cent' – or perhaps raising the prices quoted to them.

In the Lloyd's example there seems to be evidence that premiums were much too low in certain parts of the insurance market, resulting in an *overall* loss.

What should be done?

Enterprising managers can apply the 80–20 rule in a wide

Pinpointing the problem (or opportunity)

range of situations by analysing the appropriate figures. This is normally a fairly easy process, using billing figures, absenteeism records, repair costs, machine down-time and so on. For example:

- A few customers may account for most of the sales revenue. This might suggest problems such as too much reliance on a few customers. If only one or two went elsewhere the effect could be extremely damaging.

- A small number of items in a warehouse may account for a large part of the stockholding costs. Can the costs be reduced by arranging a 'call-off' system with suppliers, thus transferring to them the cost of holding the expensive items of stock?

- A large proportion of absenteeism derives from one section of the company. Having discovered this the manager can ask why. Is there something wrong in the management of the 'bad' department? Is there something wrong with the working conditions?

- More than half of the company's revenue is earned from only 5 per cent of the product range. Can profits be improved by further developing or promoting these popular products? Should some of the slow movers be discontinued and resources switched to the more successful lines? Is there a need for new products to be planned to add to the successful range, or to replace them when their heyday is over?

- 90 per cent of quality control rejects result from only one or two characteristics of the product. Does this indicate a weak point in the production process – inadequate operator training or faulty machinery? Alternatively is there a fundamental design fault?

As these examples show, the 80–20 Rule is applicable in a very wide range of situations. It is well worth looking for it whenever problems arise or opportunities are sought.

Another real-life example

A company in the financial field prided itself on the importance of a major client who provided about 25 per cent of the company's revenue. This client was personally serviced (part-time) by the Chairman and to a greater extent by a departmental manager. These executives were backed up by a team of more junior staff who specialised entirely in the client's business.

At a time when profits were falling, an O & M analysis was made which showed that whilst the important client provided 25 per cent of the revenue, servicing the business consumed about 30 per cent of the total costs. The business, which was held in such high regard, actually resulted in a loss!

The 80–20 Rule analysis which led to this discovery caused the company successfully to renegotiate terms with the client *and* find ways to make the servicing more efficient. Savings were made by introducing some mechnisation in the paperwork and cutting out some obsolete forms, records and checking processes.

Prior to the 80–20 analysis no one had the slightest inkling that a problem existed.

Footnote

Vilfredo Pareto – an Italian economist – was probably the first person to formally state the 80–20 rule. Resulting from studies of the distribution of wealth and later observations in other areas he stated:

> 'In any series of elements to be controlled a selected small fraction in terms of number of elements almost always accounts for a large fraction in terms of effect.'

In other words, most of the problem is caused by a small part. Find the small part and the problem can be solved.

25

ACTIVITY SAMPLING – FINDING OUT WHAT REALLY GOES ON

Activity sampling is a technique developed in the heyday of work measurement techniques and is probably the only one which is of any real use. One reason why activity sampling works is that it does not involve evil little men with stop watches. The reason for recommending it here is that although full-scale activity sampling can take weeks to complete and involve fairly extensive mathematics it can be readily applied in a simple, shortened form useful to enterprising managers in a hurry.

Activity sampling is a first-class way to find out what goes on in an unsatisfactory area (without upsetting the staff) and to pinpoint the cause or causes of a problem.

How the simple version works

Suppose that action is required in a small department to find the cause of hold-ups or delays in the work. Extra staff will no doubt have been demanded, this being the automatically proposed solution to all such problems. There is, however, a high probability that measuring how much effort is expended on each job will show up the real cause of the problem.

IDEAS FOR ENTERPRISING MANAGERS

Step 1

Explain to *all* the staff what the problem is and that you are intending to use activity sampling to find a solution. Explain that:

- The study is not a witch hunt.

- The staff will not be observed by anyone from outside their own group.

- It is not a fault-finding expedition.

Step 2

Having obtained the willing cooperation of the staff discuss with each individual the work they do and prepare a recording form as shown:

Date:								
Activity	9.15	9.42	10.01	10.30	11.00	11.37	12.10	etc.
Filing								
Calculating costs								
Receiving phone calls								
Completing estimates								
Checking calculations								
Allocating folders								
Finding code numbers								
Miscellaneous								
Waiting for work								

Activity sampling – finding out what really goes on

Under the heading *'Activity'* should be written the *main* items of work carried out and, at the head of each column, a time of day entered which has been *taken from a table of random numbers*. It is important not to enter regular times such as on-the-hour and half-hours as this will result in unreliable results – as explained later.

Step 3

Provide each member of staff with a supply of the forms, say one for each of five days, and ask them to complete them according to the following rules:

- At the time shown at the head of the first column (9.15 a.m. in the diagram) place a tick against the work being done *at that time*. Thus, if the employee is finding code numbers the tick should be made against that activity. If, however, the employee has paused in the course of finding a code number to sharpen a pencil, or any other unlisted activity, the tick should be placed against 'miscellaneous'.

- If a time is missed by a minute or two it does not matter. The tick can be placed against the activity involved at the time the observation is actually made.

- If absent for meals, visits to the loo or other personal breaks, the column can be left blank.

- Continue through the day putting ticks in columns at the appropriate time.

Step 4

Collect the forms together (note that they have no names on them, proving that you are not witch-hunting) and add up the ticks against each activity.

Step 5

Convert the number of ticks into man-hours per activity. This can be done by calculating the total man-hours available (i.e. 10 staff × 8 hours per day × 5 days = *400 hours*) and allocating the hours according to the percentage of ticks per activity.

For example:

	Percentage of ticks	No. of hours
Filing	5	20
Calculating costs	15	60
Phone calls	10	40
Completing estimates	25	100
Checking calculations	5	20
Allocating folders	1	4
Finding code numbers	1	4
Miscellaneous	30	120
Waiting for work	8	32
Total	100	400

Step 6

Discuss the results with the staff and draw conclusions, using their experience to help you interpret the results.

Conclusions you might expect

Taking the figures in the example above it is immediately obvious that *Miscellaneous* and *Waiting for work* are high. The high number of hours for miscellaneous may mean one of the following:

- A main activity was not listed on the form. This could be due to an oversight. Alternatively an activity which is regarded as trivial is in fact a major time-consumer. If the former it may be worth redesigning the form and repeating

Activity sampling – finding out what really goes on

the exercise. If the latter you could be on to something, e.g. a chance to use a machine to speed up dreary time-consuming calculations.

- It could be that Miscellaneous includes a lot of time-consuming visits from members of the sales force chasing up estimates or endless requests for information (probably unnecessary) from the accounts department. At all events there is a prima facie opportunity for improvement.

In real life *Checking* is often a high proportion and, on close scrutiny, is often found to be unnecessary. Too much checking can often give rise to *Waiting for work* as a result of, say, a clerk being held up until the boss gets round to checking documents that the clerk needs.

A lot of time spent on filing may indicate a poor filing system. Or possibly this relatively unskilled job is being done by someone whose main purpose is, say, calculating. Delays in production may be due to filing work being allocated wrongly and a bottleneck being caused.

It is not unusual to unearth work which has somehow 'crept in' – sometimes without the manager being aware of it! A case study from real life will illustrate some of the possibilities:

The department comprised three staff engaged in production planning. The leader of the group was a 'production planner' assisted by the other staff who were essentially records and progress clerks. The problem, as presented, was confined to the planner who found it necessary to put in many hours of overtime to complete the scheduling of production resources.

The suggestion had been made that another clerk was necessary but this idea was strongly challenged by the planner's head of department. The objection was made on the grounds that the type of work the planner was overburdened with was nothing clerical. The two existing clerks could adequately cope with all the routine work which did not require specialist know-how.

IDEAS FOR ENTERPRISING MANAGERS

The possibility of splitting the planner's work was remote, as was the chance of obtaining the services of another planner to take over part of it.

Initial discussions were held between the group and an O & M analyst during which the group offered the view that no streamlining was likely to help and that the situation was simply one of under-staffing. The planner's work was then examined in broad outline with two results:

- The methods used for calculating and production planning were found to be sound and could only marginally be streamlined.

- It was shown that the planner did a certain amount of checking and signing of documents previously worked on by the two clerks.

It was concluded in discussion that action based on the findings above would be unlikely to achieve a significant improvement. It was decided to carry out activity sampling over three days to see if any useful leads could be obtained.

Observations of the planner's work were made at approximately 15-minute intervals with the following results:

- Total observations taken – 84

- Observed checking and signing – 22 (approx. 26 per cent)

- Observed using telephone – 12 (approx. 14 per cent)

- Observed planning and miscellaneous – 50 (approx. 60 per cent)

Whilst it was fully appreciated that the very small number of observations taken over a limited period could

Activity sampling – finding out what really goes on

easily be misleading the results were considered to be significant. The indications were that the planner could spend about 40 per cent of his time on work not directly related to his main function.

Even allowing for an error of exaggeration (no more likely than an error in the other direction) it would appear that an unexpectedly large amount of time was spent on the telephone and in routine checking. The planner was himself surprised at the results but did not consider the period of the observations to be untypical. He had, of course, completed his own recording form and had no lack of faith in the resulting percentages.

Guided by this evidence further studies were made of the telephone work and the routine form checking. The majority of phone calls was found to be incoming and from one department in a different location. These calls were invariably queries. They could be answered by almost anyone in the group and often did not require an immediate reply. Arrangements were made for telephone calls to be replaced by telex messages wherever possible and also for the clerks to intercept the remaining telephone calls.

Examination of the need to check forms resulted in some time-saving reorganisation of the clerical work coupled with changes in the method. Much of the checking was eliminated as unnecessary, i.e. mistakes were very rarely found.

By these means the work load on the planner was sufficiently reduced to achieve the desired objective. It is worth noting that the telephone calls coming in were found to occur on average once every nine minutes. Allowing for say, two minutes per call, plus the disturbance time it is not difficult to see how time-consuming this activity had been.

It will be noted how little observation was needed to find the root of the problem yet the subject himself was not aware of the cause of his troubles. This phenomenon is a common one – caused by being too close to the problem to see its cause.

Something to avoid

Never rely on the subject's opinion as to what percentage of his or her time is taken up by any particular activity. Studies show that these opinions are often very inaccurate. This is not because people are basically dishonest or stupid but for two main reasons:

- They are too close to the problem (as in the example above).

- Difficult or unpleasant work looms large in anyone's mind whilst easy, enjoyable work does not. For this reason we are likely to say that unattractive work taking, say, 10 per cent of our time, takes 40 per cent. Conversely, we underestimate how much time is spent on enjoyable work.

A word on random times

It is essential to use random times for observations (especially self-observation). If regular and foreseeable times are used the subject will, even unconsciously, prepare for the moment and arrange to be doing what he or she thinks is right and not the work which would come along in the normal way.

A department of about 15 people carried out a self-observation activity sampling at *regular* times – on the hour and at each quarter. The result showed that:

- No one ever went to the loo.

- No miscellaneous items ever appeared.

- No one ever had to wait for work.

A later exercise using random times gave some very different answers!

Activity sampling – finding out what really goes on

The enterprising manager will find that this technique can provide a quick and fairly painless way to find out what is going on. If a full explanation of the technique and the reason for using it is given to the staff concerned it will be found that they not only accept it but actually enjoy it. In the best situations the staff can become so involved in it that they will look for the causes of the problems themselves and come up with their own ideas for improvements.

26

FORECASTING THE LIKELIHOOD OF . . .

The world is constantly changing and many of the factors that will influence a manager's future are outside his own control. This is the best possible reason for trying to predict what is likely to happen so that problems can, as far as possible, be anticipated and minimised or opportunities exploited.

There are many (complex) statistical techniques for sales forecasting and the like but most managers are non-statisticians and need a fairly down-to-earth means of forecasting.

One relatively simple method which can provide a reasonable guide to future facts and figures involves the use of a standard deviation (SD). Once the SD has been calculated some predictions can be made based on past results. It must be noted, however, that using SD is only valid where no drastic changes to the general business environment are expected in the next few months compared with the last. If, for instance, a new competitor has entered the field with a first-rate product it is almost certain this will have an effect and last year's results will be less reliable for forecasting.

However, given that no big changes can be foreseen, using SD can be very helpful.

Forecasting the likelihood of . . .

An illustration – Accidents on the A10

Suppose a manager is responsible for planning the provision of ambulance and other emergency services on a 20-mile stretch of the A10. It would be extremely useful for him to know the likelihood of accidents occurring. Can he expect one a week or two a week? What is the chance of 10 accidents in a week – or none at all?

Assuming that we are dealing with the summer months only (the winter is likely to require a separate analysis) the first requirement is to record last year's records, and calculate the average accident rate:

Week 1	1 accident
Week 2	2 accidents
Week 3	0 accidents
Week 4	3 accidents
Week 5	0 accidents
Week 6	0 accidents
Week 7	7 accidents
Week 8	1 accident
Week 9	2 accidents
Week 10	4 accidents
Week 11	1 accident
Week 12	0 accidents
Week 13	1 accident
Week 14	2 accidents
Week 15	3 accidents
Week 16	5 accidents
Total	32 accidents
Average	2

Having worked out the average the next stage is to work out the *difference* of each figure in the table from the average. The differences are squared and the square root of the average of the squared figures is taken. The result is the SD. (This sounds horribly complicated but if taken in stages it is easy.)

Following this calculation sequence results in the accident figures working out as follows:

Accidents	Difference from average	Difference squared
1	1	1
2	0	0
0	2	4
3	1	1
0	2	4
0	2	4
7	5	25
1	1	1
2	0	0
4	2	4
1	1	1
0	2	4
1	1	1
0	2	4
3	1	1
5	3	9
		TOTAL 60

Average 2.

Average = 60 ÷ 16 = 3.75
Square root of 3.75 = 1.9
SD = 1.9.

Statisticians have shown that 68 per cent of occurrences or values will fall within a range of 1 SD above or below the average for the group of occurrences or values; 95 per cent will fall within the range of 2 SD's from the average; and 99.7 per cent within 3 SD's from the average. Based on this, to make a prediction about accidents in the future the SD is applied to the average of the previous results as follows:

- 68 per cent of the future summer weeks can be expected to have accidents within the range of the average plus or minus 1 SD (= 2 plus or minus 1.9). In other words, the manager can expect to have to deal with 0 to 4 accidents in 2 weeks out of every 3 (rounding to 'whole accidents').

- 95 per cent of future summer weeks can be expected to

Forecasting the likelihood of . . .

produce accidents within the range of the average plus or minus 2 SD's (i.e. 2 plus or minus 3.8). In other words, in most weeks he should be prepared for anything between 0 and 6 accidents (rounded figures).

- 99.7 per cent of weeks will show an accident rate of average plus or minus 3 SD's (i.e. 2 plus or minus 5.7). In other words, to be as certain as he can reasonably expect to be he should gear up for up to 8 accidents each week.

The example chosen is a deliberately simple one with figures selected to make it easy to follow the calculations. On the face of it the same conclusions could be reached merely by inspection of the past record and without any calculation at all. However, real-life figures for sales, production, absenteeism, breakages and so on are usually a little too complicated to come to a sensible conclusion without some form of analysis. Standard Deviation is one of the easiest methods available.

Note for the mathematically minded

More information on SD can be obtained from *Statistics Without Tears*, a Pelican paperback by Derek Raintree. This book, subtitled 'a primer for non-mathematicians', offers information useful to managers on a whole range of statistical techniques.

27

SPOTTING THE TREND

There are many statistical techniques for forecasting future trends, results, costs, and numbers of all kinds. One of these, regression analysis, is used to spot trends and requires a fair amount of mathematics. However, the *principle* behind the mathematics can be used by the non-mathematical enterprising manager to obtain a rough idea of how things are going.

Suppose, for example, that records have been kept of sales, absenteeism, accidents, machine breakdown or whatever. The manager often wants to know the answer to the question 'is it getting better or worse?' The figures themselves may give the answer immediately without need for any statistical analysis. If sales have doubled each month for the past 20 months the manager knows perfectly well how things are going. However, in real life the answer is rarely so conveniently obvious.

Figures tend to fluctuate, with a good month following a bad one and random fluctuations cropping up from period to period. In such a situation there may be an underlying trend which is hidden by the fluctuations and occasional wild figures. Such trends can be spotted with the help of a transparent ruler, a sheet of graph paper and the regression analysis principle.

Spotting the trend

Using the transparent ruler

The figures in question should be plotted on a graph to show the scatter, e.g.

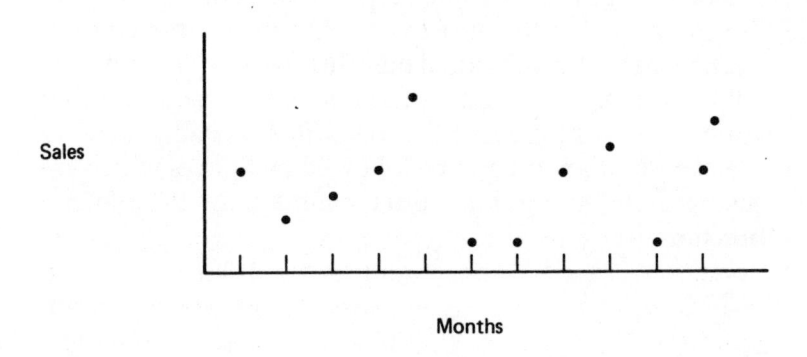

[Graph showing Sales vs Months with scattered dots]

A transparent plastic ruler is then placed on the graph with the edge placed roughly mid-way through the dots. The ruler can then be moved up, down or turned until its edge forms a line through the middle. Roughly half the dots will be on either side of the edge after allowing a little extra weighting for the odd maverick dot.

A pencil line can then be drawn along the ruler edge giving an approximate average trend. In the diagram shown the trend line would be slightly upwards from left to right indicating that although the monthly sales are irregular the *general* direction is upwards. Continuing along the trend line will not of course necessarily amount to an accurate forecast of sales in the next month!

Accuracy can be increased by removing any very wild figures for which there is a clear explanation. For example, sales may have dropped to an all-time low in the month that the warehouse burned down. This is (hopefully) a rare event and unlikely to be repeated so it is probably safe to exclude the figures for the month of the fire.

Why 'regression'?

People unfamiliar with the term 'regression analysis' are often puzzled when first introduced to it. The everyday meaning of regression is 'going backwards' whilst in this instance it is apparently referring to a trend into the future. The answer lies in the principle behind the mathematics. If a trend exists, the individual monthly figures (or whatever) will tend to regress towards the line of the trend. In other words, the wildly adrift figures will inevitably tend to cancel each other out and be followed by figures which are closer to the trend line, thus maintaining the general direction.

The moving average

A modest amount of arithmetic is required to work out a moving average – another means to spot a trend. The moving average is calculated by averaging a series of values (such as the last 12 months' sales figures) and, in each successive month, dropping the oldest figure and bringing in the latest figure. The theory is that the oldest figures will be less representative of the current situation than the newer ones. Replacing the oldest with the newest will reflect this. At the same time the fluctuations which may occur from month to month are smoothed out by this method so that the general trend is made clearer.

Thus it might be found, for example, that the average monthly sales for the previous 12 months were as follows:

January	20.1 tonnes
February	20.2 tonnes
March	21.0 tonnes
April	21.1 tonnes
May	21.3 tonnes, etc.

These averages indicate a fairly steady upward trend even if one or two months out of those in the previous 12 months showed a fall from the average or a fall from the month which preceded them.

The historigram

The historigram (not to be confused with a histogram) is a form of bar chart which visually illustrates trends over a period of time. An example is shown below:

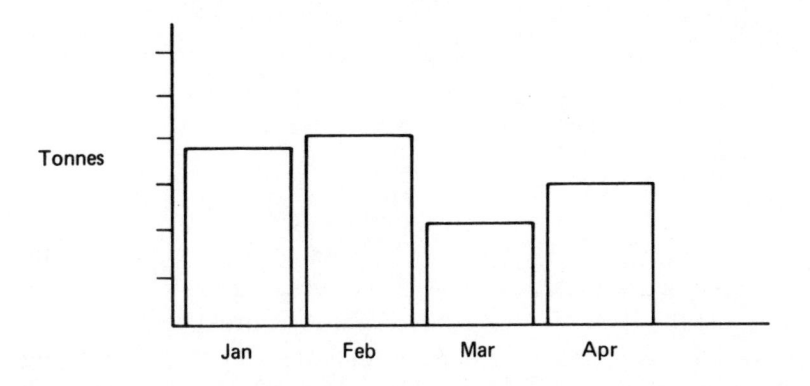

This very simple device can be used as a visual aid – for example, by placing it where all members of the department can see it. The visible results of the department's work, sales, output or whatever can add interest to everyone's work and act as a powerful stimulus.

Further reading

For those with a more mathematical mind who may be interested in a more sophisticated treatment of regression analysis, a useful source of information is *Statistics Without Tears* by Derek Rowntree (Pelican). The book also describes techniques for sampling, analysing relationships (correlation) and other statistical tools which may be of use to the enterprising manager.

Various types of bar chart (and other diagrammatic ways to spot trends) are described in the Video Arts booklet *Choosing and Using Charts* by Gene Zelazny. This booklet also provides examples of line graphs and a number of ways they can be used in business.

INDEX

A and B-reader system, 152–3
Action plan, appraisal, 93
Activity sampling, 175 *et seq.*
Appraisal schemes, 87 *et seq.*
Authority, clarity in, 51
Average, moving, 188

Brainstorming, 36 *et seq.*
Break-even point, 163 *et seq.*

Centralisation, 52–3
Charts, paperwork, 137
Commando squad, 47
Communication, 20–3, 51, 54
Computers, 55, 61
   and errors, 143
Control, procedure, 20
   and planning, 25 *et seq.*
   systems, 33
Cost control, 62 *et seq.*
Creativity, 36 *et seq.*

Decentralisation, 52–3
Decision-making, 41 *et seq.*
Delegation, 45, 110 *et seq.*
Discipline, 155 *et seq.*

Emergency cover, 46
Enterprising manager,
   definition, 7
Equipment, 18

Errors, clerical, 143 *et seq.*
Extended line structure, 51

Feedback, systems, 33–5
Fixed costs, 163–4, 167
Forecasting, 29, 182 *et seq.*
Forms, 127 *et seq.*
   and contents, 128–9
   and purpose, 128
   consultation on, 134–5
   design, 129–34
Free stock, 60

Group size, 46

Hawthorn effect, 53
Historigram, 189

ICI, 59
Ideas, evaluation, 38–40
Instructions, vague, 147
Interview, appraisal, 88 *et seq.*
   checklist, 84
   technique, 84–5
   post interview analysis, 86
   selection, 83–5
Invoice checking, 63–4

Job conditions, 11, 12, 13
Job description, 19, 80, 102

Leadership style, 15
Likert, Rensis, 16
Lloyds, 170

Manpower, 19
Mechanisation, checklist, 151
　office, 148 *et seq.*
　possible benefits, 149
　possible disadvantages, 150
Meetings, price of, 73 *et seq.*
Methods, 18
Milward, G. E., 127

O & M, questions, 137
Objectives, 17, 29
　and training, 101
On-job training, 99 *et seq.*
Order quantity, 60
Organisational structure, 17, 44 *et seq.*

Pareto's Principle, 170 *et seq.*
Pareto, Vilfredo, 172
Parkinsonism, 110
Parkinson's Law, 114
Person profile, 80–2
Physical conditions, 12
Planning and control, 25 *et seq.*
Plans, developing, 31
Problems, help with, 23
　solving, 36 *et seq.*, 66 *et seq.*
Profile, person, 80–3
Promotion, 14

Random times and sampling, 175, 180
Recruitment, 14
Regression analysis, 186–8
Reports, cutting down, 154 *et seq.*
Responsibility, and authority, 19
　clarity in, 51

Rules, 115–18

Salaries, 14
Selling price, 168
Simulation technique, 66 *et seq.*
Skills, 14
Span of command, 45
Specialisation and organisation, 48
Staff, selection, 79 *et seq.*
　turnover, 144–5
Standard deviation, 182–5
Stock records, 58 *et seq.*
Structure, divisional, functional, 47–50
　in a small department, 55
Supervision and errors, 143–4
System and errors, 145

Telephone technique, 123
Time, and the manager, 120 *et seq.*
　and planning, 27
　and reading, 152 *et seq.*
　and training, 104
Timing and implementation of change, 39–40
Training, and benefits of, 96–8
　assessing needs, 101
　on job, 99 *et seq.*
Trends, 186 *et seq.*

Variable costs, 163–4, 168
Visual stock control, 58–61

Work, allocation, 19
　conditions, 146
　distribution, 145

X-Chart, 129